M000306401

Be prepared...
To learn...
To succeed...

Get **REA**dy. It all starts here.
REA's preparation for the ELA is **fully aligned** with
New York State's Learning Standards.

Visit us online at
www.rea.com

READY, SET, GO!

New York

ELA

Grade 8
English Language Arts

Staff of Research & Education Association

Research & Education Association
Visit our website at
www.rea.com

The Learning Standards presented in this book were created and implemented by the New York State Education Department (NYSED). For further information, visit the NYSED website at *www.emsc.nysed.gov/3-8/e-home.htm.*

"Funnel Web" photo (p. 69) by Amit Kulkarni
"Sheet Web" photo (p. 70) by Alan Bauer
"Space Colonization" photo (p. 119) courtesy NASA

Research & Education Association
61 Ethel Road West
Piscataway, New Jersey 08854
E-mail: info@rea.com

Ready, Set, Go!
New York State ELA, Grade 8

Printed in the United States of America

Library of Congress Control Number 2005934545

International Standard Book Number 0-7386-0096-2

REA® is a registered trademark of
Research & Education Association, Inc.

TABLE OF CONTENTS

About Research & Education Association

Founded in 1959, Research & Education Association is dedicated to publishing the finest and most effective educational materials—including software, study guides, and test preps—for students in middle school, high school, college, graduate school, and beyond. Today, REA's wide-ranging catalog is a leading resource for teachers, students, and professionals.

We invite you to visit us at *www.rea.com* to find out how "REA is making the world smarter."

Acknowledgments

We would like to thank Larry B. Kling, Vice President, Editorial, for his editorial direction; Pam Weston, Vice President, Publishing, for setting the quality standards for production integrity and managing the publication to completion; Christine Reilley, Senior Editor, for project management; Diane Goldschmidt, Associate Editor, for post-production quality assurance; Christine Saul, Senior Graphic Artist, for cover design; Jeremy Rech, Graphic Artist, for interior page design; and Jeff LoBalbo, Senior Graphic Artist, for post-production file mapping.

We also gratefully acknowledge the writers, educators, and editors of REA, Northeast Editing, and Publication Services for content development, editorial guidance, and final review.

SUCCEEDING ON THE NYS GRADE 8 ENGLISH LANGUAGE ARTS TEST

ABOUT THIS BOOK

This book provides excellent preparation for the New York State (NYS) Testing Program Grade 8 English Language Arts (ELA) test. Inside you will find lessons, drills, strategies, and test practice—all of it with a single-minded focus: success on the ELA test.

We have also made every effort to make the book easy to read and navigate.

This book is divided into several parts. The first section is a **PRETEST**, which is half the length of an actual NYS Grade 8 ELA test and introduces students to some of the sections on the actual test, including:

- an informational passage

- a poem

- a Web page for an Internet site about a student organization

- two informational articles, which will be read to practice for the listening portion of the test

- a writing prompt instructing students to write an original essay

Following the pretest is a **lesson section**, which teaches students about the different types of test questions, step by step. A full-length **POSTTEST**, which matches the content and structure of the NYS Grade 8 ELA test, appears at the end of the book. An answer key with detailed explanations of each answer is provided.

HOW TO USE THIS BOOK

FOR STUDENTS: To make getting through the book as easy as possible, we've included icons shown on the next page that highlight sections like lessons, questions, and answers. You'll find that our practice tests are very much like the actual ELA you'll encounter on test day. The best way to prepare for a test is to practice, so we've included drills with answers throughout the book, and our two practice tests include detailed answers.

FOR PARENTS: New York State has created grade-appropriate Learning Standards that are listed in the table in this introduction. Students need to meet these standards as measured by the ELA. Our book will help your child review for the test and prepare for the exams. It includes review sections, drills, and two practice tests complete with explanations to help your child focus on the areas he/she needs to work on to help master the test.

FOR TEACHERS: No doubt, you are already familiar with the ELA and its format. Begin by assigning students the pretest. An answer key and detailed explanations follow the pretest. Then work through each of the lessons in succession. When students have completed the subject review, they should move on to the posttest. Answers and answer explanations follow the posttest.

ICONS EXPLAINED

Icons make navigating through the book easier by highlighting sections like lessons, questions, and answers as explained below:

 Question

 Answer

 Tip

 Lesson

 Activity

 Writing Task

WHY STUDENTS ARE REQUIRED TO TAKE THE ELA

In 1996 the New York State Regents approved 28 Learning Standards in seven content areas that define New York's expectations for student learning. To determine how well a student is advancing and whether the student is on course to perform well in high school, eighth grade students are required to take the ELA.

It is one of the key tools used to identify students who need additional instruction to master the knowledge and skills detailed in the Learning Standards, which guide education in New York State.

WHAT'S ON THE ELA

The NYS Grade 8 ELA test is given in two sessions on two days. The format and time restrictions are as follows:

Day 1
Session 1: Part 1
Reading selections and 25 multiple-choice questions
45 minutes, plus an additional 5 minutes of prep time

Session 1: Part 2
Listening selection and short-response and extended-response questions
45 minutes, plus an additional 5–10 minutes of prep time

Day 2
Session 2
Reading selections and short-response and extended-response questions
Independent writing prompt
90 minutes, plus an additional 5 minutes of prep time

Questions

Multiple-choice questions on this test contain four response options, one of which is correct. The short-response and extended-response questions require students to write (rather than select) an appropriate response. Students will be asked to demonstrate their understanding of a listening selection and some reading selections by providing written text-based answers. The independent writing prompt is an open-ended question that requires students to demonstrate their writing proficiency.

LEARNING STANDARDS*

Questions on the test are based on the following New York State Learning Standards:

Standard 1: Students will read, write, listen, and speak for **information and understanding**.

	Page Numbers
● Use text to understand vocabulary	27
● Understand stated information	43
● Compare and contrast information	61
● Categorize information	61
● Draw conclusions and make inferences	110

Standard 2: Students will read, write, listen, and speak for **literary response and expression**.

	Page Numbers
● Identify main idea or theme	43
● Identify author's point of view/purpose	77
● Recognize how author's language use creates feelings	77
● Identify cultural values	77
● Identify genre	77
● Interpret theme	93
● Interpret characters	93
● Interpret plot	93
● Determine use of literary device	93

*The Learning Standards presented in this table were created and implemented by the New York State Education Department (NYSED). For further information, visit the NYSED website at *www.emsc.nysed.gov/3-8/e-home.htm.*

Standard 3: Students will read, write, listen, and speak for **critical analysis and evaluation.**

	Page Numbers
• Recognize point of view	77
• Use critical analysis to evaluate information	130
• Use critical analysis to evaluate ideas	130
• Use critical analysis to recognize point of view	130
• Distinguish between fact and opinion	130

Standard 4: Students will read, write, listen, and speak for **social interaction.**

	Page Number
	147

TIPS FOR THE STUDENT

Students can do plenty of things before and during the actual test to improve their test-taking performance. The good thing is that most of the tips described in the following pages are easy!

Preparing for the Test

Test Anxiety

Do you get nervous when your teacher talks about taking a test? A certain amount of anxiety is normal and it actually may help you prepare better for the test by getting you motivated. But too much anxiety is a bad thing and may keep you from properly preparing for the test. Here are some things to consider that may help relieve test anxiety:

- Share how you are feeling with your parents and your teachers. They may have ways of helping you deal with how you are feeling.

- Keep on top of your game. Are you behind in your homework and class assignments? A lot of your classwork-related anxiety and stress will simply go away if you keep up with your homework assignments and classwork. And then you can focus on the test with a clearer mind.

- Relax. Take a deep breath or two. You should do this especially if you get anxious while taking the test.

Study Tips & Taking the Test

- **Learn the Test's Format.** Don't be surprised. By taking a practice test ahead of time you'll know what the test looks like, how much time you will have, how many questions there are, and what kinds of questions are going to appear on it. Knowing ahead of time is much better than being surprised.

- **Read the Entire Question.** Pay attention to what kind of answer a question or word problem is looking for. Reread the question if it does not make sense to you, and try to note the parts of the question needed for figuring out the right answer.

- **Read All the Answers.** On a multiple-choice test, the right answer could also be the last answer. You won't know unless you read all the possible answers to a question.

- **It's Not a Guessing Game.** If you don't know the answer to a question, don't make an uneducated guess. And don't randomly pick just any answer either. As you read over each possible answer to a question, note any answers which are obviously wrong. Each obviously wrong answer you identify and eliminate greatly improves your chances at selecting the right answer.

- **Don't Get Stuck on Questions.** Don't spend too much time on any one question. Doing this takes away time from the other questions. Work on the easier questions first. Skip the really hard questions and come back to them if there is still enough time.

- **Accuracy Counts.** Make sure you record your answer in the correct space on your answer sheet. Fixing mistakes only takes time away from you.

- **Finished Early?** Use this time wisely and double-check your answers.

Sound Advice for Test Day

The Night Before. Getting a good night's rest keeps your mind sharp and focused for the test.

The Morning of the Test. Have a good breakfast. Dress in comfortable clothes. Keep in mind that you don't want to be too hot or too cold while taking the test. Get to school on time. Give yourself time to gather your thoughts and calm down before the test begins.

Three Steps for Taking the Test

1) **READ.** Read the entire question and then read all the possible answers.

2) **ANSWER.** Answer the easier questions first and then go back to the more difficult questions.

3) **DOUBLE-CHECK.** Go back and check your work if time permits.

TIPS FOR PARENTS

- Encourage your child to take responsibility for homework and class assignments. Help your child create a study schedule. Mark the test's date on a family calendar as a reminder for both of you.

- Talk to your child's teachers. Ask them for progress reports on an ongoing basis.

- Commend your child's study and test successes. Praise your child for successfully following a study schedule, for doing homework, and for any work done well.

- Test Anxiety. Your child may experience nervousness or anxiety about the test. You may even be anxious, too. Here are some helpful tips on dealing with a child's test anxiety:

  - Talk about the test openly and positively with your child. An ongoing dialogue not only can relieve your child's anxieties but also serves as a progress report of how your child feels about the test.

  - Form realistic expectations of your child's testing abilities.

  - Be a "Test Cheerleader." Your encouragement to do his or her best on the test can alleviate your child's test anxiety.

PRETEST

Part 1: Reading

*D*irections

The following article describes how Chinese-Americans entered the country through Angel Island in California in the 1800s and 1900s. Read "Chinese Immigration to Angel Island." Then answer questions 1 through 5 on the answer sheet on page 23.

Chinese *Immigration* *To Angel Island*

In the 1800s and 1900s, immigrants flocked to America to escape poverty and oppression and enjoy a better life in "the land of the free." Most of these immigrants were processed, or registered, at an immigration center on Ellis Island in New York City, but those entering the country through California were processed at an immigration center on Angel Island in the San Francisco Bay. Many of these immigrants were from China.

The immigration stations on Ellis and Angel Islands differed in that Angel Island was actually a detention center. While immigrants processed on Ellis Island waited hours or days to enter America, those processed on Angel Island were forced to wait weeks or months. A shortage of jobs in the West and racial prejudice were to blame. A series of discriminatory laws were passed that made it difficult for Asians to enter the United States. The Chinese were the most seriously affected by these laws.

More than seventy percent of immigrants detained on Angel Island were Chinese.

Many Chinese initially immigrated to America in search of gold in California, which they nicknamed the "Gold Mountain." They were soon to uncover the fallacy of the "Gold Mountain," however, as they were met with resentment and suspicion from Americans and forced to work menial jobs for little pay. These first immigrants laid railroad tracks, reclaimed swamp land, worked as migrant farmers, and labored in the fishing and mining industries. While they toiled away for long hours under treacherous working conditions, many still remained optimistic about the future and were grateful to be in America, where they were free.

I told myself that going by this way would be easy.
Who was to know that I would be imprisoned at Devil's Pass?
How was anyone to know that my dwelling place would be a prison?

Go On

A new detention center opened on Angel Island in 1910, and its location, which was even more isolated than the first, was considered ideal for interrogations. This new center had space for more detainees and regular boat service to the mainland. Over the next thirty years, 175,000 Chinese immigrants were detained there. To express their feelings of loneliness and fear of brutality and deportation, some detainees carved poetry into the wooden walls of the detention center, some of which is still visible today. Wrote one detainee:

America has power, but not justice.
In prison, we were victimized as if we were guilty.
Given no opportunity to explain, it was really brutal.

Despite being mistreated, the Chinese permitted to live in America made great contributions to their new country. They supplied labor to American factories, especially during the Civil War when laborers were in short supply. Some Chinese-American entrepreneurs started their own businesses, which sparked the American economy. Using their advanced agricultural knowledge, Chinese-Americans in the West converted what was once useless land into rich farming soil, making the West self-sufficient and no longer dependent upon the East for food. Chinese immigrants brought with them their language, beautiful writing, culture, and customs, which were eventually integrated into American society.

The United States abandoned the detention center on Angel Island in 1940, when "Chinese Exclusion Acts" were repealed and a fire destroyed the administration building. A museum has been established in the old detention center, so visitors can see what life was like for these early Americans. The Angel Island Immigration Station Foundation (AIISF), a non-profit group of concerned individuals and descendants of Chinese-Americans once detained on Angel Island, hopes to preserve and restore the immigration station, which they consider an important part of American history.

Go On

1 Why does the author quote lines from poetry carved into the walls of the detention center on Angel Island?

(A) She wants to show how the Chinese felt about their detainment.

B She wants to emphasize that the Chinese were there a long time.

C She wants to prove that the Chinese on Angel Island were mistreated.

D She wants to show that the Chinese detained on Angel Island were artistic.

2 The Angel Island registration center can best be described as

~~F~~ larger than the registration center on Ellis Island.

(G) more frightening than the registration center on Ellis Island.

~~H~~ easier to access than the registration center on Ellis Island.

J more frequently used than the registration center on Ellis Island.

3 The author of this passage writes that ... "some Chinese who were already settled in America were cruelly deported to impoverished imperial China." What does *impoverished* mean?

(A) poor

B distant

C dangerous

D populated

4 Why do people today consider the Angel Island registration center important?

F It is a popular tourist attraction.

(G) It is an important part of American history.

H It proves that the Chinese were treated unfairly.

J It shows the contributions of the Chinese in America.

5 It is likely that the creators of the second detention center on Angel Island intended to—

A process more Chinese

(B) detain and deport more Chinese

~~C~~ assist more Chinese entering America

~~D~~ discourage Chinese from entering the country

Go On

Directions

Read "Daffodils" by William Wordsworth. Then answer questions 6 through 10 on the answer sheet on page 23.

Daffodils
by William Wordsworth

I wander'd lonely as a cloud
That floats on high o'er vales and hills,
When all at once I saw a crowd,
A host, of golden daffodils;
Beside the lake, beneath the trees,
Fluttering and dancing in the breeze.

Continuous as the stars that shine
And twinkle on the Milky Way,
They stretch'd in never-ending line
Along the margin of a bay:
Ten thousand saw I at a glance,
Tossing their heads in sprightly dance.

The waves beside them danced; but they
Out-did the sparkling waves in glee:
A poet could not but be gay,
In such a jocund company:
I gazed—and gazed—but little thought
What wealth the show to me had brought:

For oft, when on my couch I lie
In vacant or in pensive mood,
They flash upon that inward eye
Which is the bliss of solitude;
And then my heart with pleasure fills,
And dances with the daffodils.

Go On

6 Which excerpt from the poem uses personification, the literary technique that gives objects or things human qualities?

F "They flash upon that inward eye"

G "They stretch'd in never-ending line"

H "And then my heart with pleasure fills"

J "Tossing their heads in a sprightly dance"

7 Which statement best expresses the main idea of the poem?

A Cherish happy times.

B Appreciate the beauty of nature.

C Remember the good and let go of the bad.

D Today's experiences can be remembered tomorrow.

8 The style and working of the poem show that the poet is

F giving advice about living life.

G remembering a beautiful sight.

H celebrating the coming of spring.

J describing how he feels when alone.

9 What is the source of the poet's pleasure in the last stanza of the poem?

A a sight

B solitude

C pictures

D a memory

10 The author of the poem writes, "For oft, when on my couch I lie/In vacant or in pensive mood . . ." What does the word *pensive* mean?

F angry

G empty

H thoughtful

J disappointed

Go On

Directions

Look at the Web page for an Internet site about a student organization. Then answer questions 11 to 13 on the answer sheet on page 23.

Join Us!

Join Us!

Past Projects

Meetings Photos

Activities Calendar

National Groups

Environmental News

Save Our Earth Youth Network

Save Our Earth Youth Network is a non-profit organization consisting of students in 45 schools throughout the state of New York. The Network strives to raise awareness about environmental hazards, such as ground, air, and water pollution, and turn this awareness into positive action. Students who are part of the network work together to promote recycling, increase the number of trees planted in New York each year, reduce pollution, and support habitat conservation for endangered animal species in New York and throughout the world. Students make friends, help the earth, and make memories that will last a lifetime.

Become a Member!

Join the Save Our Earth Youth Network and learn what students in nearby schools are doing to protect their environment and increase the public's awareness of environmental hazards. Become involved in upcoming Save Our Earth Youth Network events—they're fun! The Network meets at least once a month, more often when a project is underway. To become a member of the Save Our Earth Youth Network, simply fill out the registration form below and click Send. A representative will contact you before the next meeting.

Last Name:

First Name:

Address:

Phone:

School:

Grade:

City:

E-mail:

⬤ SEND　　⬤ CLEAR FORM

Go On

11 The service provided by this Web site is mainly intended to

A persuade students to work to save the earth

B inform students about important environmental issues

C describe what students can do to help the environment

D encourage students to join an environmental organization

12 The Web site is effective because the author

F supports her position with details

G makes being part of the group sound like fun

H writes on behalf of students from many schools

J explains the importance of working to save the earth

13 All of the following is required for registration EXCEPT

A E-mail

B Grade

C School

D Teacher

STOP

Part 2: Listening and Writing

Directions

In this part of the test, you will listen to two articles: "Martha Washington" and "Mount Vernon." Then you will answer some questions to show how well you understood what was read.

For this practice test, ask a parent or friend to read the articles aloud twice. As you listen carefully, you may take notes on the articles during the readings. You may use these notes to answer the questions that follow. Use the space on pages 12 and 13 for your notes.

These articles are about Martha Washington, the first First Lady of the United States, and Mount Vernon, the beloved estate of George and Martha Washington.

Go On

Martha Washington

When George Washington took office as the president of the United States in 1789, his wife Martha became the first of the First Ladies. The daughter of a plantation owner, Martha assumed her new duties with grace and dignity. Her years as First Lady, however, were neither the best nor worst years of her life.

Martha Dandridge was a petite, dark-haired girl of eighteen when she married a wealthy colonist named Daniel Custis. She gave birth to four children, but lost two when they were just babies. When her surviving two children were very young, her husband died unexpectedly, leaving her a widow at the age of twenty-six.

Martha's days became brighter two years later when she was introduced to tall, handsome Colonel Washington. Everyone wanted young George Washington to visit their homes in those days because he had acquired quite a reputation for his military accomplishments. When traveling through Virginia, he was persuaded to visit a wealthy friend's mansion in order to meet a charming woman named Martha. They enjoyed each other's company immensely and were married within the year.

Even though George's mansion, named Mount Vernon, was their official home and where Martha preferred to be, Martha often traveled with her military husband. In 1775, she stayed with him at his headquarters in Massachusetts, and then followed him to New York. In the spring of 1777, she spent time with him in New Jersey. The next winter, Martha followed her husband to Valley Forge, Pennsylvania. In the years following, she traveled to visit him several more times. A homebody at heart, her trips reflected her bravery and determination to support her husband during difficult times.

When George Washington became president, he and Martha entertained government officials from Europe. Their gatherings were very formal because George and Martha wanted the United States to be respected and accepted by the governments of Europe. Martha ran their presidential homes in Philadelphia and New York with poise and good judgment.

When George's presidency was over, he and Martha retired to Mount Vernon along the Potomac River, where they shared many enjoyable days with family, friends, and guests. While living at Mount Vernon, the first president and First Lady received many visitors and dignitaries from all over the world. Though Martha had devoted her life to being a strong helpmate to her husband, she protected their privacy by burning their personal letters before she died. Martha Washington is remembered not only as the first First Lady, but as a woman who was determined to be supportive of her husband, whether on a battlefield or by his side at their cherished Mount Vernon home.

Go On

Mount Vernon

Mount Vernon was George and Martha Washington's cherished home for many years.

Spanning eight thousand acres, Mount Vernon was actually five fully functional farms, each with its own buildings and staff. The main farmhouse where the Washingtons lived was known as the Mansion, and was renovated by raising the original roof to make the house two stories high. Several additions were also added, including a piazza where the Washingtons and their guests enjoyed a beautiful view of the Potomac.

With lavish gardens gracing most of the property, Washington carefully designed the entire estate with a keen eye for the landscape and scenery. The entrance roads for the Washingtons and their guests wound east and west through the property, while the working areas and outbuildings of the farm were situated along roads leading north and south.

Running such a massive plantation was no easy task. Cooking, cleaning, laundry, butchering, and gardening were endless. Washington wanted Mount Vernon to be as self-sufficient as possible—if it could be made or grown on the property, it was. Items that couldn't be created onsite were bought and stored on the grounds. Outbuildings such as the storehouse, smokehouse, salthouse, laundry, spinning room, greenhouse, shoemaker's house, overseers' quarters, and servants' quarters were buzzed with activity. Many servants spent long hours caring for the needs of the many family members and guests who stayed with the Washingtons.

Much of Mount Vernon's self-sufficiency depended upon well-managed crops and livestock. Large amounts of hay and firewood were needed. Fish were netted from the Potomac and were preserved in barrels using salt. Livestock was raised not only for the ham, pork, mutton, and veal, but Washington bred sheep to produce wool for spinning into yarn for clothing. Flax and hemp were planted for producing linen and rope.

One of Washington's prized outbuildings was his enormous greenhouse. Washington loved to grow tropical and semi-tropical plants such as coffee, orange, lemon, and lime. These plants needed warmth provided by an adjoining stove room, where a servant kept a large fire burning to heat the greenhouse.

George Washington was an excellent horseman and took great pride in his stable and horses. Washington used horses for traveling and touring his grounds, as well as for racing and fox hunting. Washington not only broke and trained his own horses, but also bred some of the best mules in the country. Washington used mules, which are crossbreeds between female horses and male donkeys, as draft animals for much of the work on the plantation.

Whether the Washingtons were riding along the lanes of their plantation or strolling through the gardens surrounding the mansion, they enjoyed the forethought and vision George Washington had for a serene estate with breathtaking views in every direction.

Go On

Notes

Notes

14 Complete the chart below by writing three character traits that best describe Martha Washington. Then provide a detail from the article to support each trait.

Character Trait	Supporting Detail

15 In what ways was Mount Vernon "self-sufficient"? Use details from the article to support your answer.

_____

_____

_____

_____

_____

Go On

16   **Martha Washington once said these words:**

> *"I am still determined to be cheerful and happy, in whatever situation I may be; for I have also learned from experience that the greater part of our happiness or misery depends upon our dispositions, and not upon our circumstances."*

Use information from both articles to explain what the quotation means and why Martha Washington held this view.

_____

_____

_____

_____

_____

_____

Go On

Planning Page

You may **PLAN** your writing for Number 17 here if you wish.

17

> Describe what a dinner visit at George Washington's Mount Vernon estate might have been like when George and Martha Washington lived there.
>
> In your answer, be sure to include
>
> - features of the home and grounds of the estate
> - a description of Martha Washington's character
> - information from BOTH articles

Check your writing for correct spelling, grammar, and punctuation.

_____

_____

_____

_____

_____

_____

_____

_____

_____

_____

_____

_____

_____

Go On

Directions

In this part of the test, you will be writing an original essay. Follow the directions on the next two pages and begin your writing on page 21.

Go On

Planning Page

You may PLAN your writing for Number 18 here if you wish, but do NOT write your final answer on this page. Your writing on this Planning Page will NOT count toward your final score. Write your final answer on pages 21 through 22.

18

> The role of First Lady has changed since Martha Washington moved into the White House. Write and article for your school newspaper in which you discuss how you think the role of First Lady has changed.
>
> In your article, be sure to include
>
> • how you think the role of First Lady has changed
>
> • why you think these changes have occurred
>
> • details to make your writing interesting

Check your writing for correct spelling, grammar, and punctuation.

_____

_____

_____

_____

_____

_____

_____

_____

_____

_____

_____

Go On

STOP

MARKING INSTRUCTIONS

Make heavy BLACK marks.
Erase cleanly.
Make no stray marks.

CORRECT
MARK

INCORRECT
MARK

Multiple-choice questions

1. (A) (B) (C) (D)

2. (F) (G) (H) (J)

3. (A) (B) (C) (D)

4. (F) (G) (H) (J)

5. (A) (B) (C) (D)

6. (F) (G) (H) (J)

7. (A) (B) (C) (D)

8. (F) (G) (H) (J)

9. (A) (B) (C) (D)

10. (F) (G) (H) (J)

11. (A) (B) (C) (D)

12. (F) (G) (H) (J)

13. (A) (B) (C) (D)

Student Name_____

Pretest—Part 1

1. **A** draw conclusions and make inferences

    The author quotes lines from the poetry carved in the wall of the detention center on Angel Island to show how the Chinese felt about being detained. The other answer choices do not closely relate to the information revealed in the quotations.

2. **G** compare and contrast information

    You have to compare the two registration centers to answer this question. Answer choice B is correct. Since immigrants were detained (imprisoned) much longer in the registration center on Angel Island, it was more frightening than the registration center on Ellis Island.

3. **A** use text to understand vocabulary

    The word impoverished means poor. Many Chinese left their country because they could not find employment. Therefore, you can tell from the context that imperial China was very poor.

4. **G** draw conclusions and make inferences

    People today are working hard to restore the registration on Angel Island because it is part of America's history. By visiting the center, people can more closely imagine and appreciate what early immigrants experienced.

5. **B** draw conclusions and make inferences

    The second detention center was larger and the author said its creators liked its isolated location, which implies that some Chinese were brutally interrogated in an effort to deport them. Answer choice B is the best answer.

6. **J** determine the use of a literary device

    This question asks you to identify an answer choice using personification. The correct answer is A: "Tossing their heads in a sprightly dance." This line gives daffodils human qualities.

7. **B** identify main idea

    Answer choice B best expresses the main idea of the poem. The poet is appreciating the beauty of nature. It is the only answer choice that refers to nature, an important theme of the poem.

8. **G** determine the use of a literary device

    This question asks you about the style of the poem. You can tell from the style of the poem that the author is remembering something he saw. The correct answer choice is G.

9. **D** understanding stated information

    The source of the poet's pleasure in the last stanza is a memory. Answer choice D is the correct answer.

10. **H** use text to understand vocabulary

    The word pensive means thoughtful. The poet says he lies on his couch in a vacant or pensive mood. He implies that these words have opposite meanings. If his mind is vacant, it is empty. Pensive would mean the opposite of vacant.

11. **D** identify author's point of view/purpose

    The author wrote the content on this Web site to encourage students to join the organization. The author tries to make the group sound fun and uses an exclamation point after "Become a member!" This helps you determine the correct answer.

12. **B** use critical analysis

To answer this question, you have to analyze the Web site and determine why it is effective. The best answer choice is that the author makes becoming a member of the group sound fun. If the group's activities sounded boring, no one would want to join.

13. **D** understand stated information

The answer to this question is on the Web site. You need to choose the answer choice that is not required for registration. This is D: teacher.

Pretest—Part 2

14.

Character Trait	Supporting Detail
1. supportive	She traveled with her husband even though she wanted to stay home.
2. strong	She started a new life after the death of her first husband.
3. personable	She entertained many people at Mount Vernon.

15. **Sample answer:** Mount Vernon was self-sufficient in that Washington believed whatever could be made or grown there should be made or grown there. The large staff grew most of the food and cared for the grounds. Only food that could not be grown there was bought and stored until it was needed.

16. **Sample answer:** The quotation means that Martha kept a positive outlook and tried to look on the bright side. Even though she lost some of her children and her husband, she remarried and started a new life. She traveled with her military husband, though she said she was a homebody and liked to stay at Mount Vernon, the large estate owned by her husband that she considered home.

17. **Sample answer:** Dinner at Mount Vernon during the time of Martha and George Washington was probably an elegant experience. Martha and George entertained often and even dined formally with government officials. They probably used their large staff to cater to guests' needs in a massive formal dining room. The food eaten was probably grown on the estate and the meal would be delicious. After the meal, Martha and George would probably ask their guests to relax on the piazza and enjoy a beautiful view of the Potomac.

18. **Sample answer:** The role of First Lady has changed a great deal since Martha Washington moved into the White House. Martha mainly spent her time hosting social events and traveling around the world with her husband. Her main role was to be supportive, of the President and everyone who entered the White House.

    Today, it is acceptable for a First Lady to be much more involved in decision-making and even to oversee issues related to the government. This is because the role of women in general has changed since Martha Washington's time. Today, it is acceptable for women to assume high-level managerial positions. When Bill Clinton was President, First Lady Hillary Clinton was very involved in running the American government. She oversaw the revision of some children's programs and is now a senator in New York. Perhaps the biggest change in being a "First Lady" is yet to come. It is entirely plausible that during your lifetime a woman will run and be elected President. Then the "First Lady" will be a "First Man."

 Lesson 1: Vocabulary

New York State Learning Standard:

S1 Information and Understanding

Subskills:

Use text to understand vocabulary (S1)

Vocabulary questions

To answer questions about vocabulary, you may have to figure out the meaning of a word from its **context**, or the way it is used in a sentence. Sometimes you will know the meaning of a word. When this happens, however, you need to make sure that the definition you are choosing fits the way the word is being used. As you know, some words have more than one meaning. You need to choose the meaning based on how the word is used. When you don't know the meaning of a word, you can often find clues to a word's meaning from looking at the surrounding sentences.

Activity

Break into four groups. Use a dictionary to look up the definition of each of the words assigned to your group. Then, with your group members, write a story/paragraph using each of the words.

When all groups have finished, read the story out loud. (Be sure to pronounce each word correctly!) See if your classmates can guess the meaning of each word based on its context.

Group 1	**Group 2**	**Group 3**	**Group 4**
好身份	胡说	留心	味住的
muliebrity	tommyrot	hearken	sipid
无赖	极好子的	沉默寡言的	透明的
yob	skookum	farouche	limpid
有齿的	金钱的	迎将	飞跳的
dentigerous	pecuniary	zugzwang	saltant
狂走也	偏母遗传	酋长	有害的
amok	matrocliny	sachem	malefica
透明的	十路退	自以为聪明者	衰老的
luculent	katabasis	wiseacre	senescent

transparent

Passage 1

Now read this passage and then answer the questions that follow.

The Birth of Golf
by Nathan Barrett

In the 1400s, farmers in eastern Scotland invented a simple but ingenious new pastime. It was a sport that required only simple, easily improvised equipment: sticks and round pebbles. This sport was perfectly suited to the geography of the Scottish coast, which included grassy tracks, sand dunes, and rabbit holes. The makeshift entertainment would evolve over generations into the game we know today as golf.

This early form of golf had an immediate impact on the people of Scotland. It was immensely popular among the citizens, who were so enthusiastic about the game that they devoted much of their time to it. They spent so much time playing golf, in fact, that they neglected their duty to King James II by shrugging off their obligation to train for the military. The enraged king, seeing that his military might suffer because of his people were spending all of their time playing with sticks and pebbles, declared golf illegal in 1457.

The outlook for the new sport brightened again almost fifty years later, when King James IV discovered that the banned pastime was actually quite entertaining. Not only did he lift the ban, but his interest in the sport—like a celebrity endorsement today—made golf more popular than ever. The royalty of England and Scotland began teaching foreign rulers how to golf.

The sport took hold in France, but the heart of golf remained in Scotland. The capital of the country, Edinburgh, hosted the world's most famous golf course, which was called Leith. In 1744, the first golfers' organization, the Gentleman Golfers, formed at Leith. They originated the idea of golf tournaments, yearly competitions featuring impressive trophy prizes. Additionally, they devised a set of rules for the game that were widely accepted.

Golf has come a long way since the sticks and stones used in the 1400s. By the 1700s, specially designed clubs and balls were being handcrafted by exclusive shops. Club handles were made mostly from special kinds of wood. Many early clubs also had heads made of wood, though some heads were made of blacksmith-forged iron. Today, most clubs are made entirely of lightweight, super-strong metal. Even with these improvements, golf in the modern era is essentially the same game Scottish farmers played six hundred years ago.

 Questions

1. Reread the first paragraph of the passage. What does the word *makeshift* mean?

临时的

_____

_____

2. Read this sentence from the passage.

"In the 1400s, farmers in eastern Scotland invented a simple but ingenious new pastime."

What do you think the word *ingenious* means?

有独创性的

_____

_____

3. The passage states, "The outlook for the new sport brightened again almost fifty years later, when King James IV discovered that the banned pastime was actually quite entertaining."

Write a word that means the same as the word *banned*.

_____

Check your answers on the next page.

Passage 1: "The Birth of Golf"

 Answers

1. **Sample answer:** Makeshift entertainment means spur-of-the-moment entertainment or entertainment that was made up quickly.

2. **Sample answer:** The word *ingenious* means clever or imaginative.

3. **Sample answers:** *forbidden, outlawed, illegal.*

Passage 2

Read the following poem. When you finish reading, answer the questions that follow.

My November Guest
by Robert Frost

MY Sorrow, when she's here with me,
Thinks these dark days of autumn rain
Are beautiful as days can be;
She loves the bare, the withered tree;
She walks the sodden pasture lane.
Her pleasure will not let me stay.
She talks and I am fain to list:
She's glad the birds are gone away,
She's glad her simple worsted gray
Is silver now with clinging mist.
The desolate, deserted trees,
The faded earth, the heavy sky,
The beauties she so truly sees,
She thinks I have no eye for these,
And vexes me for reason why.
Not yesterday I learned to know
The love of bare November days
Before the coming of the snow,
But it were vain to tell her so,
And they are better for her praise.

Questions

1. When the author writes "She walks the sodden pasture lane," the word *sodden* refers to

   A   wet
   B   bright
   C   sunny
   D   green

Tip

Go back and find this line in the poem. What time of year is it?

2. The author writes that Sorrow talks but he is "fain" to listen. What does *fain* mean?

   (F) obliged
   G   afraid
   H   reluctant
   J   irritated

Tip

Think about how the author feels about what Sorrow is saying. Does he listen? How does he feel about listening?

3. The author writes, "She thinks I have no eye for these/And vexes me for reason why." What does *vexes* mean?

   A   invites
   B   pesters
   C   explains
   D   questions

Tip

What is the tone in these lines? Is Sorrow asking him nicely? Or annoying him?

Now check your answers on the next page. Read the explanations after each answer.

Passage 2: "My November Guest"

 Answers

1. A   The word *sodden* means wet. It is November, the fall, and everything is gray and dreary. The pasture is not bright, sunny, or green in November.

2. F   In this sentence, the word *fain* means obliged. The speaker politely listens to Sorrow speak, although he does not agree with what she is saying.

3. B   Answer choice B, *pesters*, is the best answer choice here. While she might invite or question him for a reason why, *pesters* better matches the tone of these lines. She is annoying him by demanding an answer.

Passage 3

Read this passage and answer the questions that follow. Use the tips under each question to help you choose the best answer.

Amazing Morocco

Morocco is a land of sights and smells. In fact, it's hard to describe Morocco without painting a picture filled with vibrant reds, oranges, and yellows. Add the heady aromas of spices, and you'll begin to get a sense of this vibrant country. Everywhere you turn, your senses are nearly overwhelmed with sights and sounds and smells.

The colorful country of Morocco is located in northern Africa, touching both the Atlantic Ocean and the Mediterranean Sea. It also shares borders with the countries of Algeria and Western Sahara. If you look on a map, you might be surprised to see that a section Morocco's shoreline nearly touches Spain. Morocco's closeness to Spain is reflected in much of its culture. France has had a great deal of influence on Morocco as well.

Most Moroccans speak Arabic, and many educated people in the cities speak French and sometimes Spanish. The original Moroccans were Berbers, a non-Arab African tribe of people who have subsisted in the area for thousands of years. Nearly ninety percent of Moroccans today are either entirely or partially of Berber descent. Arabs are the second largest group of people living within Morocco and have influenced much of Moroccan culture, including religion. There are also nearly 100,000 French people living in Morocco.

For many years, the Berbers roamed in the Moroccan countryside, speaking their own language and passing their history from generation to generation by telling stories. Today, many Berbers are mixed into the Arab mainstream culture. Though some Berbers still live in rural areas raising livestock and growing crops, many are educated and have jobs in the cities.

If you travel to Morocco from Spain, you will take just a short boat ride to the city of Tangiers. This closeness to Spain is what gives Tangiers its nickname, the Gateway to Morocco. Tangiers is a coastal city with breathtaking views and that it is a first stop for many tourists from all over the world.

As you travel inland, you'll arrive at the historic city of Fez. This city was built on the crossroads of old caravan paths. Fez is a very religious city and carries on the great traditions of Islam. It is the home of treasured mosques, which are the churches of the Islamic religion.

Traveling down the Atlantic coast, you'll come to the city of Rabat, which is the capital of Morocco. Rabat was the capital of Morocco under French rule and remains the capital of the country. Rabat is the official residence of the Moroccan king. Rabat is also home to a large university and a school of music, dance, and theater arts. Rabat is connected to its sister city Salé by a bridge over the river that separates the cities.

Just a little farther down the Atlantic coast of Morocco is the famous city of Casablanca, which is the largest city in Morocco. Casablanca is the business capital of Morocco and is a large center for foreign trade and banking. While the French were in control of Casablanca, they built the largest man-made harbor, which helped the Moroccans to buy and sell products with Europe.

In the southern part of Morocco is the city of Marrakech. Nowhere are the colors and smells of Morocco stronger and more powerful than in Marrakech. Many merchants sell handmade goods here and the leather products and woven carpets are among the finest in the world. Arabs and Berbers alike come to sell their goods and sip mint tea in the blazing sunlight.

Life in Morocco is a mix of old traditions and modern ways. Within Moroccan cities, there are the remaining old cities, called medinas. Medina streets are narrow mazes that connect the gated courtyards of private homes with the central marketplaces. Many courtyards are filled with trees and flowers and fountains. Moroccan people living in these old sections of the cities use their courtyards for sewing, weaving, eating meals, and visiting neighbors. You'll find many children in the narrow streets carrying water to their homes or bread to be baked in the ovens down the street. The marketplaces of Morocco are filled with strange and amazing sights. Besides the merchants selling their carpets and spices, there are dancers and musicians, acrobats and magicians, and even snake charmers.

 Questions

1. The author writes, "it's hard to describe Morocco without painting a picture filled with vibrant reds, oranges, and yellows." What does the word *vibrant* mean?

充满生气的

A   pale
B   clear
C   bright
D   mixed

 Tip

What point is the author trying to make about Morocco? Read the last sentence of the first paragraph if you're not sure.

2. Read this sentence from the passage.

The original Moroccans were Berbers, a non-Arab African tribe of people who have subsisted in the area for thousands of years.   → exsisted

In this sentence, what does *subsisted* mean?

存在

F   lived
G   endured 忍耐
H   traveled
J   breathed

 Tip

Eliminate incorrect answer choices. Then consider the point the author is trying to make.

3. The author writes, " Today, many Berbers are mixed into the Arab mainstream culture." What does the word *mainstream* mean?

A   minority 主流的
B   ordinary 普通的
C   noticeable
D   exceptional 特殊的

Check your answers on the next page.

Passage 3: "Amazing Morocco"

 Answers

1. C   In the first paragraph of the essay, the author is trying to make the point that everything in Morocco is rich and strong. The colors are bright. While clear might also be the answer, it is not the best answer.

2. F   *Subsisted*, as it is used here, means lived. The Berbers have lived in the area for thousands of years.

3. B   *Mainstream* means normal or ordinary, so answer choice B is correct. The other answer choices don't fit the context as well; the point of the sentence is that the Berbers have mixed their culture into the Arab culture, so that it is now mainstream or ordinary.

Passage 4

Read the following passage. Then answer the questions at the end of the passage.

The Common Cold: Unbeatable Bug?

While the human race has accomplished many amazing feats, curing the common cold has not been one of them. Even after hundreds of years of research, scientists still cannot stomp out the tiny bug.

Nearly everyone knows the miserable feeling of having a cold. The sickness can affect your entire head with symptoms including sneezing, coughing, a blocked or runny nose, a sore throat, and a headache. Some especially nasty colds carry along all of these symptoms.

A cold can really disrupt your life. Every year, millions of people miss work or school due to colds. This hurts the economy and the educational system. People spend billions of dollars each year for medicines to reduce their nagging symptoms. So far, no medicine has been proven beyond a doubt to work, however.

The term "cold" is actually just a label for a group of symptoms. These symptoms are actually caused by viruses, microscopic parasites that rely on other organisms to live. When these viruses find a good host—you, for instance—they thrive, but end up giving you some sort of disease in return. Talk about ungrateful guests!

However, in the case of a cold, the disease itself isn't usually what bothers you. The most annoying symptoms are actually caused by your own immune system, which does everything it can to eradicate the virus. The immune system will produce extra mucus to try to flush out the virus through the nose or to trap it and take it to the stomach, where it will be killed with stomach acid. This mucus, of course, results in the cold's most infamous symptom: the runny nose. The stuffy head symptom is caused by inflammation of blood vessels above the nose. Sneezing and coughing are brought about by the irritation caused by the immune system's defense mechanisms. Coughing, in particular, occurs when the irritation moves to the lungs.

Perhaps the only good thing about this cycle of discomfort is that it usually results in success within a week or so. The virus dies and is flushed away, and good health returns. Most people, however, still lament the fact that colds last as long as they do.

Throughout history, people have tried hundreds of different remedies in order to shorten the durations of their cold symptoms. Even powerful leaders like Napoleon Bonaparte concerned themselves with their nasal health. Napoleon had a recipe for cold pills that he claimed worked wonders for him— this recipe included such peculiar ingredients as "ipecacuanha root," "squill root," "gum ammoniac," and "gum arabic." Other old-time recipes called for almonds, currants, poppy seeds, or licorice.

Remedies like these may sound funny today, but we have to be humble because we haven't found a surefire remedy, either. Many scientists today believe that certain kinds of zinc, a substance often used in vitamins, provide our best hope for relief. Chicken soup is always a safe bet, too.

Scientists agree that the best way to avoid the nuisance of a cold is to avoid catching the cold in the first place. Cold viruses are transmitted from person to person. Contrary to popular belief, colds are not caused by cold weather. Going outside on a wintry day will not make you any more likely to catch a cold. There are several different reasons that people usually get colds during the colder months. The main reason is that, in the winter, more people stay indoors and end up in close contact with one another.

The virus is usually transmitted by way of people's hands. That transfer doesn't only happen when people shake hands. It can also happen through objects that are touched by several people. For instance, if someone coughs on his or her hand and then touches a doorknob, the next person to touch the door-knob may pick up a virus. This transfer is practically unavoidable, so the best thing to do is simply to wash your hands. Also, you can try not to touch your nose or eyes, because they're easy landing zones for cold viruses, which take up residence in the cells inside the nose.

Although there are ways to reduce your exposure to colds, some scientists believe Americans suffer through as many as a billion colds per year. There's no relief in sight. For now, the common cold remains an unbeatable bug.

 **Questions**

1. Read the sentence below.

    The most annoying symptoms are actually caused by your own immune system, which does every-thing it can to eradicate the virus.

    What does the word *eradicate* mean in this sentence?

    A   get rid of
    B   surround
    C   create with
    D   absorb

 Tip

If you don't know what this word means, read the sentence carefully. Think about what the article said about the immune system's role in dealing with viruses. What does your immune system want to do with the virus?

2. The author writes that "the cold's most infamous symptom" is the runny nose. What does *infamous* mean?

   F   painful

   G   well-known

   H   long-lasting

   J   bothersome

Tip

Go back to the passage and read the sentences around this one. What point is the author trying to make?

3. Read this sentence.

Most people, however, still lament the fact that colds last as long as they do.

What does the word *lament* mean?

   A   express

   B   complain

   C   will not accept

   D   cannot believe

Tip

How do people feel about a cold lasting a long time?

4. The author writes that people still "haven't found a surefire remedy" for the common cold. What does the word *surefire* mean?

   F   medication

   G   vaccination

   H   readily available

   J   completely effective

Check your answers on the next page.

Passage 4: "The Common Cold: Unbeatable Bug?"

 Answers

1. A   The word *eradicate,* as used in the sample sentence, means to get rid of something. The immune system does not want to surround, create, or absorb the virus. It wants to eradicate it—get rid of it—completely.

2. G   The word *infamous* means well-known. The runny nose is the symptom most commonly associated with the common cold. While the answer choice "bothersome" also seems to be correct, this is not the point the author is trying to make. It helps to read the context, the sentences around the one containing the world.

3. B   *Lament*, in this instance, means complain. People complain about how long a cold lasts. While answer choice D might also be acceptable, answer choice B is the better answer.

4. J   A "surefire remedy" is completely effective and would get rid of all of the cold's symptoms. Answer choice J is the best answer. While some of the other answer choices seem acceptable, they don't fit the context as well as answer choice J.

Lesson 2: Main Idea

New York State Learning Standards:

S1 Information and Understanding

S2 Literary Response and Expression

Subskills:

Identify main idea or theme (S2)

Understand stated information (S1)

What is the main idea?

The main idea is the essential message of a passage. Sometimes the main idea is stated in a passage, meaning you can actually put your finger on a sentence or two expressing the main idea. Other times the main idea is not stated and you have to determine it from the information in the passage.

The **theme** of a literary passage is its message or what the author is trying to say in a short story or poem. The theme is similar to the main idea.

Supporting details are **stated information** that explain and expand upon the main idea. They provide more information about the main idea. Supporting details might be facts, examples, or description.

Test questions about the main idea might ask you what the passage is mostly about or to choose the best summary of a passage. Questions about theme might ask you to choose a sentence that best states the theme. Questions about stated information in the passage simply ask you about details in the passage. You can usually go back and reread the passage to find the answers to these questions.

 # Activity

Write a paragraph, essay, or short story using one of the following quotations as the main idea. Use the graphic organizer below to help you get started. Write a quotation in the center box.

"The report of my death was an exaggeration."
Mark Twain (1835–1910)

"There are no secrets to success. It is the result of preparation, hard work, and learning from failure."
Colin Powell (1937–)

"A slip of the foot you may soon recover, but a slip of the tongue you may never get over."
Benjamin Franklin (1706–1790)

"My mother had a great deal of trouble with me, but I think she enjoyed it."
Mark Twain (1835–1910)

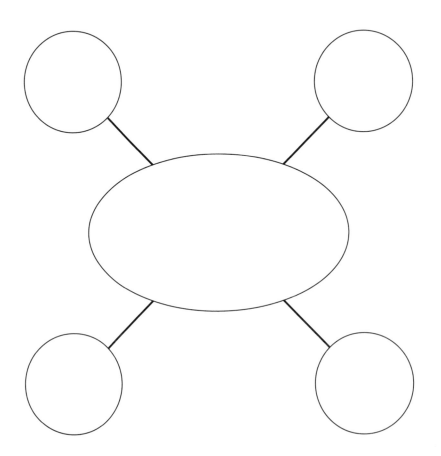

Passage 1

Now read this passage. Think about the main idea as you read. Then answer the questions that follow.

The Trail of Tears

The United States signed the Declaration of Independence in 1776. Soon after, the nation began to grow by leaps and bounds. Both population and territories increased. As European settlers explored new lands and pushed further into the frontier, they forced many Native Americans out of their homelands. By 1830, settlers had flooded into Georgia and increased the population of the state several times over. The Cherokee Indians were also living in Georgia at the time and had lived there for many years.

For a while, the settlers and the Cherokee shared the land and resided together peacefully. The Cherokee adapted to the European way of life that the settlers brought with them to America. The discovery of gold on Cherokee lands, however, prompted the settlers to urge the United States government to remove the Cherokee from their homeland. The removal of Native American people from their home territories created more space for settlers and allowed them to take control of the valuable resources found on the land. Such "removal" was quite common during this time as many other Native Americans had been forced to move west of the Mississippi River. While the removal was good for the settlers, it was devastating for the Native Americans.

In 1835, a small group of Cherokee leaders signed the Treaty of Enchota. Even though most of the Cherokee disagreed with the treaty, it allowed President Andrew Jackson to order the removal of the Cherokee from their lands in Georgia to areas west of the Mississippi. In 1838, General Winfield Scott and seven thousand men began removing the Cherokee from their homeland. The troops gathered Cherokee men, women, and children in shabby camps with little shelter and food. Then, they forced the Cherokee to march one thousand miles from Georgia to Oklahoma during the fall and winter of 1838. Many of the Cherokee fell ill or died along the way. Troops did not allow time to stop and grieve for lost loved ones, causing the Cherokee to label their march "*Nunna dual Tsuny*," or "The Trail of Tears." By the time the Cherokee reached Oklahoma, they had lost more than four thousand of their friends, relatives, and loved ones. It was one of the saddest events in the United States' brief history.

 Questions

1. Write a phrase telling what this passage is mostly about.

    The removal of Native American.

    _____

2. Now, write a sentence expressing the main idea of this passage.

   U.S. government forced Cherokee Indians move to Oklahoma.

3. Identify three supporting details (stated information) in the passage.

   The removal was good for the settlers but it was devastating for the NA.
   When they arrived, more than four thousand people died.

Check your answers on the next page.

   The removal was during the fall and winter of 1838

Passage 1: "The Trail of Tears"

 Answers

1. Your answer should contain a phrase such as "trail of tears," or "Native Americans forced to move."

2. Your answer should contain a sentence stating what the passage is about, such as "The passage is mostly about the Cherokee being forced to move to Oklahoma and the pain they suffered during this move."

3. Remember that supporting details expand upon the main idea. Here are some supporting details, but there are others!

    a. The settlers urged the Unites States government to remove the Cherokee from their homeland when they discovered gold on the land.

    b. The removal was good for the settlers, but it was terrible for the Cherokee.

    c. When the Cherokee reached Oklahoma, they had lost more than four thousand of their loved ones.

Passage 2

Read this poem. Think about its main idea as you read. When you finish reading the poem, answer the questions that follow.

Because I Could Not Stop for Death
Emily Dickinson

Because I could not stop for Death—
He kindly stopped for me—
The Carriage held but just Ourselves—
And Immortality.

We slowly drove—He knew no haste
And I had put away
My labor and my leisure too,
For His Civility—

We passed the School, where Children strove
At Recess—in the Ring—
We passed the Fields of Gazing Grain—
We passed the Setting Sun—

Or rather—He passed us—
The Dews drew quivering and chill—
For only Gossamer, my Gown—
My Tippet—only Tulle—

We paused before a House that seemed
A Swelling of the Ground—
The Roof was scarcely visible—
The Cornice—in the Ground—

Since then— 'tis Centuries—and yet
Feels shorter than the Day
I first surmised the Horses' Heads
Were toward Eternity—

 Questions

1. This poem is mostly about

    A   how a woman learns that she is not immortal
    B   a woman who takes a carriage ride with a polite man
    ⓒ   how death comes for a woman who did not expect it
    D   a woman who takes the time to remember the events of her life

 Tip

   This question asks you the main idea of the poem. Reread the title of the poem.
   Who stops for the woman? Why do you think she could not stop for Death?

2. What does the woman pass after the Fields of Gazing Grain?

    F   a Ring
    G   some Children
    Ⓗ   the Setting Sun
    J   a School

 Tip

   Go back to the poem and find the stanza where the speaker mentions the Fields of
   Gazing Grain. Then find what she passes next.

3. Where does the woman think she is headed at first?

    Ⓐ   Eternity
    B   Immortality
    C   the School
    D   a Cornice in the Ground

 Tip

   Reread the end of the poem. The woman says that centuries have passed. When she
   says "I first surmised the Horses' Heads Were toward Eternity," she means that this
   is where she first thought she was going.

Check your answers on the next page. Be sure to read the explanation after each answer.

MAIN IDEA   **Lesson 2**

Passage 2: "Because I could not stop for Death"

Answers

1. C   While several of the answer choices seem as if they are correct, only one answer choice expresses the main idea of the poem: answer choice C. The woman, the speaker of the poem, says that she was too busy to stop for death, but that death kindly stopped for her.

2. H   The answer to this question is stated in the poem. Answer choice H is the answer that appears immediately after the Fields of Gazing Grain.

3. A   You need to reread the end of the poem to find this answer. It is stated in the poem.

Passage 3

Read this passage. Think about its main idea as you read. When you finish reading the passage, answer the questions that follow.

Mosquitoes: Annoying but Amazing

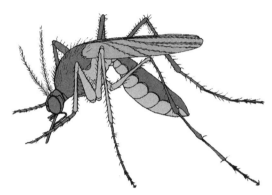

While the warm, sunny weather makes outdoor activities, such as picnics, swimming, parades, and sporting events enjoyable, pesky mosquitoes may be lurking nearby eager to interfere with your fun. Mosquitoes are tiny little creatures that bite people, make them itch, and sometimes even transmit diseases. While mosquitoes are annoying and sometimes hazardous, they are also fascinating little pests.

Little Flies
Of all the insects, the mosquito is most similar to the fly. They both have wings, compound eyes, and three main body segments: a head, a thorax, and an abdomen. Basically, the mosquito is a skinny fly with longer legs and a tube (called a proboscis, pronounced pra-BAH-sis) for a mouth. In fact, the word "mosquito" is Spanish for "little fly."

These "little flies" are highly advanced and specialized creatures. More than two thousand types of mosquitoes live in the world and they've been around for over thirty million years—far longer than humans. Over the millennia, mosquitoes have developed a wide range of abilities, which help them survive and make them difficult to outsmart.

Incredible Senses
Mosquitoes' greatest abilities are their acute senses, which they use to find food. Their main sensors specialize in detecting three things: chemicals, visual cues (color and motion), and heat.

Mosquitoes can smell the chemicals that people and animals give off when they breathe and sweat. Mosquitoes can find these chemicals in the air from as far as one hundred feet away! As they close in on their target, mosquitoes use their compound eyes to see motion and color. Then, at the closest range, they can sense the body heat of their intended victim and can tell just where to go to find the best meal. Their three main sensors make them incredible parasites.

Once they find a source of food, they have a strange and famous way of eating—bloodsucking. They poke their tiny, sharp proboscises into people and animals and take tiny sips of blood. Don't worry about losing your blood, though, because the amount a mosquito can drink is so miniscule that you won't even notice its absence.

Don't Scratch!
The most annoying thing about mosquito bites is that they itch. This itching is caused by anticoagulants, chemicals that the mosquito uses to prevent your blood from clotting. (The bug knows that if your blood

dries quickly near the bite, it won't be able to drink additional blood.) Your body reacts to the anticoagulants by swelling the area around the bite. The result is an itchy bump called a wheal. While the wheal is there, your immune system is busy cleaning away the anticoagulants.

Although people have an instinct to scratch mosquito bites, your physician will tell you that this is not the best idea. Scratching can damage the skin or cause the bite to become infected. The best thing to do is to just wash a mosquito bite with soap and water and apply anti-itch medicine.

Beat the Bug

Mosquito bites are seldom dangerous but it is best to avoid being bitten whenever possible. Mosquitoes have been known to carry diseases that are harmful to humans and some people are allergic to mosquitoes and may become ill if bitten.

These persistent little pests are difficult to beat, but there are several precautions which can help you avoid them. Since mosquitoes are most active during the morning and evening, you might try staying inside during those times of day. Put screens in your windows to keep them out of your house. If you do go out, wear extra clothing that covers your skin to make it harder for mosquitoes to bother you. Use mosquito repellents to confuse the insects' senses and make them pass you by.

You can aid in the reduction of the mosquito population. Mosquitoes lay their eggs in standing water, which is water that doesn't move or evaporate. Standing water might accumulate in buckets, barrels, and neglected swimming pools. You can help keep mosquitoes out of your neighborhood by getting rid of standing water.

Some scientists want to go even further to fight mosquitoes. At the Veterinary Entomology's Mosquito and Fly Research Unit in Gainesville, Florida, scientists have found a new weapon called a *baculovirus* (bah-cu-loe-VĪR-us), a kind of tiny parasite found in dead mosquitoes in Florida. The scientists hope that this parasite could be used to kill the most harmful types of mosquitoes. Someday this amazing, annoying, airborne pest may be controlled.

Questions

1. What is the primary topic of the second paragraph?

   A A mosquito is a lot like a fly.
   B The word mosquito means "little fly."
   C A mosquito has a long tube for a mouth.
   D Mosquitoes have three main body segments.

Tip

Two answer choices identify supporting details in the paragraph. The other tells a fact that is not the main idea of the paragraph. The opening sentence of the paragraph provides a clue to the correct answer.

2. According to the article, what is the main reason you should avoid scratching mosquito bites?

   F You will cause a wheal.
   G You might harm your skin.
   H You will make it itch more.
   J You might cause it to spread.

Tip

Reread the information under the subheading, "Don't Scratch!" Look for the reason why you should not scratch mosquito bites.

3. Which is NOT a way that mosquitoes find food?

    A   They see color.

    B   They see motion.

    Ⓒ   They feel vibrations.

    D   They smell chemicals.

Tip

Go back and reread the information under the subheading "Incredible Senses." Remember that you need to look for the answer choice that is not mentioned in this section.

4. How do scientists hope to reduce the mosquito population?

    F   with chemicals

    Ⓖ   with a parasite

    H   with poisoned water

    J   with strong repellents

Tip

Reread the end of the article. What weapon do scientists plan to use to beat mosquitoes?

Check your answers with those on the next page.

Passage 3: "Mosquitoes: Annoying but Amazing"

 # Answers

1. A   The second paragraph explains how a mosquito is like a fly. This is what the paragraph is mostly about. The other answer choices present supporting details in this paragraph.

2. G   The article says that you should avoid scratching mosquito bites because you might damage your skin. Therefore, answer choice G is correct.

3. C   Mosquitoes find food by using their incredible senses. They can smell the chemicals that people and animals give off when they sweat. They can do this from a hundred feet away. Once they get close to their target, they find it by using their eyes to see motion and color. Answer choice C is not mentioned in the passage, so this answer choice is correct.

4. G   Amazingly, scientists plan to introduce a parasite that can kill even the most harmful mosquitoes. Answer choice G is correct.

Passage 4

Read this passage. Think about its main idea as you read. Also try to identify important information stated in the passage. When you finish reading the passage, answer the questions that follow.

The Emerald Isle

Known for its rolling green landscape, rainy climate, and rich history, there is an island about the size of West Virginia that sits in the Atlantic Ocean and is often referred to as the "Emerald Isle." Its borders also touch the Celtic Sea and the Irish Sea, and its capital is Dublin. This island is the country called Ireland.

The island of Ireland is separated into two parts. The southern part of the country is called the Republic of Ireland, and the northern part is suitably referred to as Northern Ireland. Northern Ireland is part of the United Kingdom, a group of countries on another nearby island, including England, Scotland, and Wales, as well as a few smaller islands. While Northern Ireland is governed under British laws, the Republic of Ireland, the southern part of the island, is independent.

Much of Ireland's coast is lined with low mountains, while the middle of the island is a combination of flat plains and rolling wetlands. Ireland's landscapes have been the focus of many paintings and poems. Because water-laden coastal winds cause the weather to be very rainy all year, the country is famous for its wetlands, called bogs, where many different plants grow in rich shades of green, including many different types of clovers. According to ancient Irish history, finding a four-leaf clover hidden among the regular three-leafed variety is said to be lucky. The Irish countryside, which includes farmlands as well as bogs, is often enclosed in a dense white fog.

The earliest Irish were primarily farmers, who struggled to produce enough food to feed their families and pay farmland rent to their British landlords. Around the year 1600, the potato

crop was introduced to Irish farmers, who instantly loved the potato because it thrived in many different conditions and could feed many, many people. The potato became the most widespread food in Ireland, and its abundance enabled the population to grow. Then, in 1845, a deadly fungus spread through most of Ireland's potato crops, causing them to rot and turn black. The Irish people lost their main source of food, and the famine continued for years, causing many people to die of starvation. Some tried to eat different types of plants and grasses, while others left the country and made new lives in Canada and America, causing Ireland's population to drop drastically.

Today, Ireland has developed a healthy population of around four million. The Irish diet now includes more than just the potato, though spuds are still a popular part of many meals. Ireland is known for its stews and other dishes made from beef, lamb, and pork, often accompanied by cabbage, onions, carrots, and thick breads. Most Irish foods are warm, comforting, and perfect to eat on wet and chilly days. The Irish also pass time on rainy days with music, often played on the traditional harp, fiddle, and bagpipes, as well as dances, including the Irish jig, which has an interesting history. When Ireland fell under British rule, the British outlawed everything traditionally Irish and imposed British customs—including music and dance—on the Irish people. This meant that performing dances to Irish music was illegal. Some bagpipers were even arrested! The Irish cherished their own music and dances, and so they began to perform them in secret. Irish dance masters traveled around the countryside, residing with different families and teaching their dances to many Irish citizens so that the dances would not be forgotten. They danced the jig in farm fields, on roads, at secret schools, and even in kitchens on tabletops. They invented new dance steps and sometimes participated in secret dance competitions, where the dance master who knew the most steps would win. Sometimes a dancer's skill was tested when he was asked to perform on top of a wobbly barrel. Now the jig is performed in many different public places, and anyone can learn the steps to this famous dance.

Ireland is also known for its castles, many of which can be found in Dublin, the country's capital city. Ireland's castles are impressively large and have existed for hundreds of years. Citizens and tourists can walk through their magnificent gardens and explore the majestic castles, many of which still have furniture and other antique items belonging to their former residents. The Dublin Castle was built in the early 1200s and was home to many British leaders until as recently as 1922. The Malahide Castle, located on the seaside, is even older than the Dublin Castle and was home to members of the same family for almost 800 years. Other historic buildings in the capital city include large government buildings, an ancient prison that is no longer used, churches (called abbeys), and former homes of famous Irish writers and other artists.

Another immediate association with Ireland is the country's national holiday, Saint Patrick's Day. Saint Patrick was born around the year 385 C.E., and at this time, the Irish were a pagan people, meaning that they didn't belong to an established religion such as Christianity, Judaism, or Islam. Saint Patrick was a pagan until he reached the age of sixteen when he decided to become a Christian. He then became a bishop and set out to spread Christianity throughout Ireland, building churches and schools where the religion could be taught. He spread Christianity for thirty years before his death, and two hundred years after he started, most of Ireland was Christian. A famous story of Irish folklore tells how Saint Patrick gave a sermon from a hillside and drove all the snakes from Ireland, which is intended to explain why no snakes exist in Ireland today. While snakes probably never lived in Ireland, the story represents the banishment of paganism from the country.

Saint Patrick's Day is celebrated on March 17th because it is said that this was the date of Saint Patrick's death. While it is Ireland's national holiday, Saint Patrick's Day is also celebrated in America, Canada, Australia, Russia, Japan, and other places around the world. The Irish holiday was once solely one of religious worship, but has expanded to include festivities such as parades, fireworks, concerts, and much more. Interestingly enough, it is said that the first Saint Patrick's Day parade took place in 1700s America, when Irish soldiers marched through New York City in celebration of the patron saint of Ireland. Today, the holiday is very popular in America as well as Ireland.

 Questions

1.   What is the third paragraph of this passage mostly about?

(A)   the land in Ireland
B   the coast of Ireland
C   the wetlands in Ireland
D   the plants that grow in Ireland

 Tip

Be sure to reread the entire paragraph. Don't be confused by supporting details.

2. What part of Ireland is referred to as the Republic of Ireland?

   F   the east
   G   the west
   H   the north
   (J) the south

 Tip

Reread the second paragraph. The correct answer is stated in the passage.

3. What caused the Irish famine?

   A   a drought
   B   a lack of work
   (C) a deadly fungus
   D   a change in rulers

 Tip

Reread the section of the passage that discusses the Irish famine.

4. Which statement best expresses the main idea of the passage?

   (F) Ireland is an interesting island with a rich history.
   G   Ireland is known for its flat plains and rolling wetlands.
   H   Many of Ireland's historic castles are located in Dublin.
   J   Ireland is divided into two sections, which are ruled differently.

 Tip

Choose the answer choice that refers to the main idea of the entire passage.

Check your answers with those on the next page.

Passage 4: "The Emerald Isle"

 Answers

1. A Answer choice A is the best answer. The other answer choices refer to supporting details in the paragraph.

2. J This answer is stated in the passage. The correct answer is J. The southern part of Ireland is called the Republic of Ireland.

3. C A deadly fungus that killed off the potato crops in Ireland caused the famine. Answer choice C is the correct answer.

4. F Answer choice F is the only answer choice that refers to the entire passage. The other answer choices refer to parts of the passage.

Lesson 3: Comparison and Contrast

New York State Learning Standard:

S1 Information and Understanding

Subskill:

Compare and contrast information (S1)

Categorize information (S1)

How do you compare and contrast?

When you **compare** ideas or characters in a passage, you look for traits that are alike. When you **contrast** ideas or characters in a passage, you look for the ways in which they are different. Sometimes these similarities or differences are stated in the passage. Other times you have to read the passage carefully to determine the ways in which two ideas or characters are alike or different.

Many elements in a passage or two passages can be compared and contrasted, such as the subject of a passage or passages, the main idea, characters, organizational structures, authors' purposes, settings, writing styles, and authors' point of view.

Test questions asking you to compare and contrast might ask you what two characters have in common. They might ask you to identify the ways in which two characters are different. They might also ask you why an author makes a comparison in a passage. For example, an author might compare a character to a bird to show that the character is small and moves often and quickly. Test questions might also ask you to identify a way in which two topics in related passages are alike or different. While compare-contrast questions can be multiple-choice, they are often open-ended on the New York State test. This means you have to write out your answer to these questions.

Questions asking you to **categorize information** are very similar to compare-contrast questions. They will ask you how information is arranged in a passage and under which trait information is categorized. These questions are usually multiple-choice.

Activity

Compare and contrast two of your closest friends using the Venn diagram below. Write the ways in which your friends are similar in the part of the diagram where the circles overlap. Write the ways in which your friends are different in the outer portion of the circles.

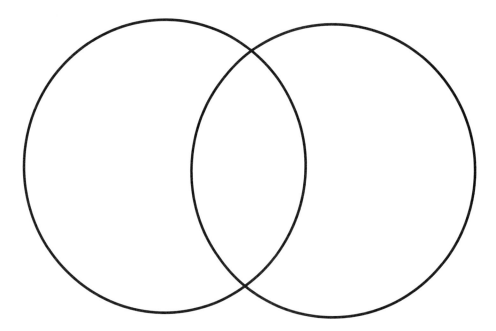

Passage 1

Now read this passage. Think about how the two characters are alike and different as you read. Then answer the questions that follow.

Clueless

Kevin pushed through the crowd to see the honor roll posted on the wall. He scanned the list quickly to find the list for eighth grade and then found his own eighth-grade class. He didn't see his name under high honors, which meant he did not get straight A's. He discovered his name under first honors, which meant his grade-point average was high, but not a perfect 4.0. The top students in the school, often dubbed the "aces" by the other students, frequently landed high honors, and they were a very bright bunch indeed. Kevin was not considered an ace, but his brother Stephen had been. While mastering new material came easy to Stephen, it was a much more difficult task for Kevin. Kevin thought that everything came easy for Stephen, who was quiet, serious, and studious. Stephen excelled at athletics, too, and he participated in just about every school club and event. He had an abundance of energy and never seemed to tire. Stephen was making his high-school debut now, impressing teachers and coaches alike. *He's so ambitious,* Kevin thought, *I wonder why I'm not like that.*

Kevin often asked his parents how two brothers could be such opposites. It was Kevin's nature to be easy-going, fun-loving, messy, clumsy, loud, and distracted by just about everything. Just the other day he caught himself observing the antics of a squirrel outside of his classroom window instead of listening to Mr. Humphrey's lecture about molecules. Athletics were such a struggle for him that he seldom bothered anymore. He just could not get his legs and arms to move the right way and most sporting events bored him anyway.

Kevin's parents seemed unsympathetic about his feelings of inadequacy. They simply told him that all people are different and that they were proud of his many accomplishments, and they, and Stephen, loved him very much. Stephen, too, never seemed to understand. Whenever Kevin would complain about feeling inferior, Stephen would bring up something Kevin was good at, like playing chess or computer games. Kevin thought his family was simply clueless about the situation.

 # Questions

1. Write a sentence describing Kevin.

   Kevin is easy-going, fun-loving, messy, clumsy, loud.

2. Write a sentence describing Stephen.

   Stephen is quiet, serious, and studious.

3. How are the two brothers different? How are they alike?

   Kevin is an active boy, and Stephen is a quiet boy. Allthough their characters are totally different, they both have good grade average.

Check your answers on the next page.

Passage 1: "Clueless"

 **Answers**

1. Your answer should contain some of Kevin's traits. Don't be afraid to draw conclusions about the characters and look beyond what is stated in the passage.

    Sample answer: Kevin is fun-loving, easy-going, messy, clumsy, loud, and easily distracted. He also seems kind and smart, but wishes he could be more like his older brother, who is very ambitious.

2. Your answer should contain some of Stephen's traits.

    Sample answer: Stephen is very smart and ambitious. He also seems kind because he tries to make Kevin feel better about himself when Kevin tells him that he feels inferior.

3. **Sample answer:** Kevin is different from Stephen because his grades are not as high. He is not as serious or athletic and he thinks he is distracted easily. He feels inferior to Stephen. Kevin and Stephen are alike in that they are both very good students. Even though Kevin does not receive straight A's, he is on the honor roll. They are also alike in that they are both kind. Kevin wants to be like Stephen, but he does not seem to resent him, and Stephen tries to make Kevin feel better about himself when Kevin tells him he feels inferior.

Passage 2

Read this passage. Think about how households today are alike and different from households of the past. When you finish reading the passage, answer the questions that follow.

Say Goodbye to the Cleavers

Households today are very different from those of the past. In the 1950s, most American families tried to model themselves after the seemingly perfect Cleavers on the television show "Leave It to Beaver." The vast majority of homes had a stay-at-home mother, who cleaned, cooked, and cared for the children, and a father who was in charge of discipline and the family finances. Fathers back then were said to have a "newspaper for a face" since they rarely interacted with their offspring unless their authority was needed. Most families had many children, and mothers strove to keep their homes as spotless and "Cleaver-like" as humanly possible. Families sat down together for a home-cooked meal each night and often had a weekly menu plan that might serve meatloaf on a particular night and fried chicken on another.

The problem with the "Cleaver ideal" is that it leaves little room for diversity, meaning not every family fits happily into this mold. Not all fathers want the responsibility of being the sole bread-winner, not all mothers are content to spend their lives working only in the home, and not all children are blessed with both a mother and a father, with many having divorced parents. Today, more than sixty percent of families in the United States have a mother who is employed outside of the home. In many of these households, both parents share in earning the family's income and in completing daily household tasks. Many modern fathers are much more involved in child-rearing than their predecessors. Their role extends far beyond discipline and includes hugs and kisses and diaper changes. While a two-parent, dual-income household may be the most common type of household today, it is certainly not the only one. According to the U.S. Census, 6.5 million single mothers work outside of the home, and a small but growing number of fathers have chosen to leave the workforce to stay at home with their young children. Fitting the modern family into an old-fashioned stereotype is like trying to put a square peg into a round hole. Americans do not want to be the Cleavers anymore.

 Questions

1. How are families today different from those of the past?

    Our parents today are different from those of the past. In past, there is usually mother stay at home and clean and cook, father works out. today, there is mother works out too. even sometimes just mother works out

 Tip

Reread the article. Underline or takes notes on the ways in which families today differ from those of the past.

2. In this article modern families are categorized by

    A   how much income they have
    B   whether they live in the United States
    C   whether both mothers and father work
    D   how much time they spend with children

 Tip

Reread the second paragraph of the passage. In what way does the author classify families today?

Now check your answers on the next page. Read the explanations after each answer.

Passage 2: "Say Goodbye to the Cleavers"

 # Answers

1. **Sample answer:** According to the article, fathers in the past were the only providers in the family, meaning they were the only ones that worked. They did not interact with their children unless discipline was needed. In most families today both the mother and father work and the fathers are much more involved in their children's lives. Both mother and father also share in household tasks, unlike in the past, when this was solely the mother's responsibility.

2. C   In the second paragraph of this article, the author says that in over sixty percent of households, both parents work. He is classifying parents in terms of whether mothers work. Answer choice C is correct.

Passage 3

Read this passage. Think about how the different types of spider webs are alike and different. Also think about how the author categorizes this information. When you finish reading the passage, answer the questions that follow.

Arachnid Addresses

 Spider webs are a familiar sight because they appear to be everywhere—in houses, in yards, on signposts, on porches, and in some unexpected places as well. Most people consider them a nuisance, but did you ever stop to closely examine a spider web? Each spider web is unique, and some are amazingly intricate. Next time you see a spider web, don't just glance at it— take a closer look!

Why does a spider make a web?
A spider's web is its residence, but it is also a snare or trap for beetles, flies, crickets, and other insects, as well as small animals such as birds and bats, which appeal to some large strong spiders. Spiders have teeth but they cannot chew, which means that they do not actually eat their prey, but drink the insect or animal's fluids instead. Not all spiders require a web to capture their prey, such as the ground-hunting wolf spider, which pursues and pounces on its prey, but many spiders do make webs, which is sometimes the only evidence that they are present at all.

Different spider species make various webs, and each is capable of producing assorted types of silk. Some spider silk is adhesive (called capture silk) and is utilized for catching insects while some is dry and used mainly to reinforce a web's strength. Different varieties of spider silk are produced and used to bind large prey before it is devoured, make a secure sac for spider eggs, or assist the spider in finding its way back to the web (called dragline silk). A spider silk strand is elastic and very sturdy when it is stretched out. It starts as a liquid, but just before it is exposed to the air, it hardens and becomes stronger than steel.

Spider silk, which is actually a protein, is produced in glands inside the spider's body called spinnerets, which weave the silken liquid into a strand that is then released into the wind where it blows onto a surface and sticks. Other spiders will produce a strand and hang from it, allowing the wind to blow the spider to its next location on the web. Once the spider has attached a sufficient amount of strands on each side, it can run across the web and rapidly move from one side to the other. Each spider web design is intricate and complicated, and some take numerous hours to make. The most common types of spider webs are orb webs, funnel webs, sheet webs, and cobwebs.

Orb Webs

The most familiar type of web is called the *orb web*. It is made by spiders such as the golden orb web spider and the garden orb web spider and is recognizable by its wheel shape. Several strands called radii (singular, radius) stem from the hub, or center of the web, and then several strands are laid over each radius in a circular pattern. This process is performed at night and can take several hours, depending on the size of the web. Some orb webs can stretch nineteen feet long and six and a half feet wide!

Constructed to catch flying insects, most of the orb web is made from sticky spider silk. When an insect is caught in the adhesive strands, it becomes entangled and struggles to get free, creating vibrations that alert the spider—which often rests in the hub—that it has snared prey. Some spiders, such as the golden orb web spider, can spin a web strong enough to catch a small bird, which often demolishes the web in an effort to break free. Most spiders are too small to eat a meal so substantial, so to prevent damage to their webs, spiders frequently leave a trail of dead insects along the web so that birds and other animals will see the web and evade it. Other spiders, however, devour large meals and will endeavor to bind the bird with silk threads so that it cannot flee. If a web is damaged in the struggle, the orb weaver spider often deconstructs the old web, regains energy on a nearby bush or tree during the day, and then rises at nighttime to build a fresh web.

Funnel Webs

The funnel web is a horizontal web, meaning it lays flat instead of extending from top to bottom. Spiders such as the Sydney funnel-web spider, found mainly in Australia, usually make funnel webs in moist, sheltered places, such as under a rock or fallen tree. Underneath the flat sheet of web is a series of funnels, or tunnels, that lead to a hole where the spider is concealed. When an insect walks on the flat web, the spider senses the vibrations, quickly emerges from the hole, bites the insect, and drags its meal back into the hole through the tunnels. Sometimes funnel web spiders hunt on the surface of the web at night, but most often they stay in the funnel because this is the

best place to remain hidden from prey. Funnel webs are very durable, and spiders that construct them often build on them for years. If you see a large funnel web, you can bet the spider inside has been around for a while.

Sheet Webs

Sheet webs are made of a perplexing maze of threads that do not appear to follow a pattern, but they are very large and effective. From the top, sheet webs look like funnel webs, but they do not have tunnels beneath. They stretch between blades of grass, plants, or trees, depending on the size of the spider. The sheet web spider also builds a net of threads above the web, so that flying insects are stopped by the net and will fall, stunned, onto the sheet. The spider, which waits below the sheet, then pulls the insect down through the sheet. When the spider is finished feasting, it repairs the damage to the sheet, which is why sheet webs can last for a long time. Some spiders, such as the poisonous black house spider, create sheets that are several layers thick.

Cobwebs

The cobweb has an even more irregular design than the sheet web. Cobwebs can often be seen in ceiling corners, but they can also be constructed on bushes and the sides of houses and barns. Like the sheet web weavers, cobweb weavers sometimes build a net above their webs to catch flying insects while the spider waits nearby or behind the web. The spider then rushes out, wraps up its victim, and feasts. Many house spiders make cobwebs, but the famous and deadly Black widow spider is also a cobweb weaver. Not all spiders are dangerous, but if you see a Black widow, stay away!

 Questions

1. How do both the golden orb web spider and the Sydney funnel-web spider know when an insect has gotten caught in their web?

    A   They feel the web moving.
    B   They feel the damage done to the web.
    C   They see it struggling through the tunnel.
    D   They hear the insect moving on the web.

 Tip

Reread the sections that discuss the golden orb web spider and the Sydney funnel-web spider. Then choose the correct answer choice.

2. In this passage, spiders are classified by

    F   the size of their webs.
    G   the way that they hunt.
    H   the appearance of their webs.
    J   the type of silk they use for a web.

 Tip

Scan the article to determine the way spiders are classified.

3. How is a funnel web different from a sheet web?

    A   It looks flat on top.
    B   It lasts a long time.
    C   It has an irregular design.
    D   It has tunnels underneath.

 Tip

Reread the description of each of these webs.

Check your answers with those on the next page.

COMPARISON AND CONTRAST   **Lesson 3**

Passage 3: "Arachnid Addresses"

 **Answers**

1. A   The passage says that both the golden orb web spider and the Sydney funnel-web spider feel vibrations on the web when an insect is caught, so answer choice A is the correct answer.

2. H   Spiders are classified by the type or appearance of their webs. Answer choice H is the best answer.

3. D   A funnel web and a sheet web look almost the same—they are both flat on top—but a funnel web has tunnels underneath. Answer choice D is the best answer.

Lesson 3   **COMPARISON AND CONTRAST**

Passage 4

Directions: For this part of Lesson 3, ask a parent or friend to read you the following two passages: "Wilson Bentley" and "The Art of a Snowflake." Then you will answer some questions about the passages.

You will listen to the passages twice. The first time you hear the passage, listen carefully but do not take notes. As you listen to each passage a second time, you may want to take notes. You may use these notes to answer the questions that follow.

Wilson Bentley

Wilson Bentley once described a snowflake as a miracle of beauty and a masterpiece of design. Bentley was a farmer who lived in Jericho, Vermont. After many attempts at using a microscope and an early camera, he became the first person to photograph a snowflake. Bentley was a self-educated young man who accomplished this historic feat in 1885 when he was just twenty years old. He went on to capture images of more than five thousand individual snowflakes, not one of which was exactly alike.

During the long, cold winters in Vermont, Bentley braved the frigid temperatures in pursuit of the exquisite beauty of snow crystals. The task was daunting, considering that snowflakes are made of many individual snow crystals, which would melt in an instant and be lost forever. Bentley assembled his equipment outdoors in order to preserve the snow crystals and capture their images on glass plates. He did this hard work not for money, but for the sheer thrill of discovering yet another brilliant image.

Bentley submitted many of his photographs and a description of his work to the Smithsonian Institute in Washington, DC. His manuscript was labeled as unscientific and was rejected. Hoping to share his findings with others, he sold individual glass plates to schools and colleges for five cents each. His work was later published by the U.S. Weather Bureau, *National Geographic*, and *Scientific American* magazine.

Wilson Bentley's neighbors fondly referred to him as "Snowflake" Bentley. Understanding the fragile, fleeting life of a snowflake, Bentley once said that "when a snowflake melted, that design was forever lost. Just that much beauty was gone, without leaving any record behind." Thanks to the curiosity and ingenuity of Snowflake Bentley, there are records of thousands of snow crystals, each reflecting a beauty like no other.

The Art of a Snowflake

When the outside air temperature is below freezing, the landscape can be transformed by millions of snowflakes, which are actually made up of billions of snow crystals.

A snow crystal is a single crystal of frozen water, shaped in an elaborate lattice pattern. Each snow crystal is created with two molecules of hydrogen for each molecule of oxygen, which is indicated by the formula, H_2O. Snow crystals can be made up of only a few water molecules but are often made up of 1000 or more water molecules. Several snow crystals are usually stuck together to form what we commonly refer to as snowflakes.

Snow crystals are created when water molecules line up in tree-like branches called stellar dendrites, which are often arranged as a hexagon. Not all snow crystals are six-sided, however. If you looked under a microscope, you would sometimes see twelve-sided snow crystals or even crystals shaped like triangles. In frigid temperatures, like at the South Pole, a snow crystal resembles a solid beveled rectangle, just like a rectangular-shaped diamond cut for jewelry.

Whether a snow crystal is a hexagon, triangle, or rectangle, its shape is nearly always symmetrical, meaning each side is very much like the others. Snow crystals can grow along flat surfaces, referred to as faceting, or into more complex shapes, referred to as branching. The facets and branches of snow crystals are created at nearly the exact same time, under the exact same conditions, which is why each branch of a snow crystal is nearly symmetrical.

There is a difference between individual snow crystals and frozen rain. While still high in the atmosphere, snow crystals are formed into intricate patterns as water molecules condense on a microscopic piece of dust. Frozen rain, or sleet, consists of single drops of water that freeze while falling to the ground. A single frozen raindrop lacks the delicate shape of a snow crystal.

Freshly fallen snow appears white; yet frozen water is often transparent. If you look very closely at individual snow crystals, they, too, appear clear. However, when snowflakes fall to the ground, they are mixed with air, leaving spaces between the flakes. When light hits a multitude of snowflakes, it bounces around among the flakes, scattering individual colors, and gets reflected back as white light.

You've probably heard that no two snowflakes are alike. Scientists say, for the most part, that's true. Since each snowflake experiences changing weather conditions as it falls, each and every snow crystal grows differently depending on wind and temperature conditions at a given moment in time. Since snow crystals follow unique paths on the way to the ground, there really are no two snowflakes that are alike.

 Questions

1. Using the chart below, describe one way that photographing a snowflake is different from photographing other objects in nature such as trees and leaves.

Different	Same
You need to use microscope to photograph a snowflake, but you don't need it for trees and leaves	

2. How is a snow crystal different from a snowflake?

    Snow crystal is much smaller than snowflake that it's made of billions of snow crystals

Check your answers on the next page.

Passage 4: "Wilson Bentley" and "The Art of a Snowflake"

 Answers

1. Fill in chart: **Sample answer:**

Different	Same
Snowflakes are difficult to photograph because, unlike other objects in nature, they melt. They are made up of many snow crystals, which form an elaborate lattice pattern with no two exactly like.	Photographing snowflakes and other aspects of involves being outside, sometimes in unfavorable weather.

2. **Sample answer:** Snow crystals have a similar shape and they appear clear when you look at them. Snowflakes are formed by many ice crystals and when light hits many snowflakes, it bounces around, and is reflected back as white light.

Lesson 4: Author's Purpose

New York State Learning Standards:

S2 Literary Response and Expression

S3 Critical Analysis and Evaluation

Subskills:

Identify author's point of view/purpose (S2)

Recognize point of view (S3)

Recognize how author's language use creates feelings (S2)

Identify cultural values (S2)

Identify genre (S2)

Most of the questions on the New York State test assessing these subskills refer to the author's purpose. Authors create pieces of writing for many reasons. They might write a short story to entertain readers or to teach a lesson. They might write an article that gives readers information or teaches them how to do something. Authors sometimes write articles or letters to convince readers to feel as they do or to persuade readers to take a certain action.

Questions about an **author's purpose** might ask you to identify the purpose of a piece of writing. You might have to decide if a passage is meant to inform, instruct, entertain, or persuade. You might also be asked what the author wants to you to think about a certain character in a story. For example, you may be asked if a character is lazy and selfish or kind and generous. You might be asked to identify a statement that the author would agree with based on a passage you have read.

You might also be asked to identify the **genre**, or the type of writing. Questions assessing genre will ask you to identify a type of writing. For example, you might be asked whether a passage is a novel, short story, or essay.

Activity 1

Determine the author's purpose for each sentence or group of sentences below. Write entertain, inform, teach, or persuade in the left-hand column.

Author's Purpose	Sentence
1.	It rained three inches yesterday.
2.	Everyone should recycle unwanted paper.
3.	Once upon a time, there lived a happy little rabbit named Bounce.
4.	Before you begin cleaning your room, you should get rid of all unnecessary clutter.
5.	The author George Eliot was actually a woman writing under a pen name.

Activity 2

In groups of 4 or 5 students, write a convincing advertisement for "Pearly White Toothpaste." Be sure to use persuasive words.

Passage 1

Think about the author's purpose as you read the following passage. Then answer the questions that follow.

How to Set up an Aquarium

Over the last century, fish have consistently been one of America's most preferred pets. Compared to most popular domestic animals, fish are low-maintenance creatures. They're well-behaved, too. It's hard to imagine a fish gnawing on furniture, shredding curtains, or shedding fur!

Setting up an aquarium can be an enjoyable project that calls on you to not only choose the conditions that would most benefit the fish, but also to make creative decisions that make the aquarium a piece of aquatic art. In order to construct an aquarium that's safe for fish and pleasing to the eye, follow these general guidelines. For more specific information, consult a specialist at your local pet shop.

What You'll Need

- Aquarium (glass or plastic)
- Water
- Filter
- Water Heater
- Water Pump
- Gravel
- Fish
- Fish Food

NOTE: Aquariums come in a wide variety of shapes and sizes, from the traditional goldfish bowl to massive tanks equitable in size to some rooms. In selecting an appropriately sized aquarium, consider how many fish you intend to keep in it. To allow your fish to live comfortably, you should generally provide at least one gallon of water per fish.

Once you've acquired the necessary materials, the first step is to cleanse the aquarium of any grime, sediments, or other refuse that may have accumulated in it. Avoid using cleaning chemicals, though, since they can contaminate the water you later add to the aquarium. Once the aquarium is clean, add gravel to the bottom, typically one pound per gallon of water. You can even accessorize your aquarium with rocks or plants.

You'll want to install a filter in order to remove contaminants from the water and keep your fish healthy. Select a filter that's suitable for the size of your aquarium, and then install it according to the directions.

The next step is to fill the aquarium with clean, cool water; a safe guideline here is to only utilize water that you would consider drinkable. Don't fill the aquarium right to the top, though, because there are still a few subsequent items you'll need to add, including the water heater and pump. Install these appliances according to their directions. Usually, the heater should be adjusted to keep the water at a temperature of about seventy-five degrees Fahrenheit.

Then the fish will be more comfortable and healthy—unless you forget to add them! The most crucial component of an aquarium is, of course, the fish. Add them to the water and enjoy your new flippered friends.

Questions

1. Why did the author write this passage?

_____

_____

_____

2. How does the author feel about fish and setting up a fish tank?

_____

_____

_____

Check your answers on the next page.

Passage 1: "How to Set up an Aquarium"

 Answers

1. **Sample answer:** The author wrote this passage to teach the reader how to set up a fish tank.

2. **Sample answer:** The author of the passage obviously likes fish. He displays enthusiasm for keeping fish as pets, and takes care to give advice to ensure that fish in a tank are comfortable and healthy.

Passage 2

Think about why the author wrote this passage as you read. Then answer the questions that follow.

Healthy Earth Hotels

People travel to escape the stresses of their daily lives, and when they visit a hotel, they expect to be able to relax in a clean, comfortable environment. Many hotels go to great lengths to pamper their guests; sometimes, however, these efforts can become excessive. For instance, hotels regularly wash bathroom towels and bed sheets every day. This leads to unnecessary usage of time, money, and resources, as well as damage to the environment. For this reason, the Healthy Earth Hotel program should be adopted by inns throughout America.

The Healthy Earth Hotel program is elementary, but highly effective. In order to implement this program, hotel operators can request a simple start-up kit which includes sturdy laminated signs and specially designed laundry hangers. These signs and hangers, when installed in each guest room, quickly and conveniently educate guests about the Healthy Earth Hotel plan and how they can utilize this plan to help safeguard the environment.

The bed sheet sign is a small laminated card that is located on the nightstand of each room. The card informs the guest that the hotel customarily changes the bed sheets every day; however, if the guest doesn't feel this is necessary, he or she can leave the card on the bed. This serves as a signal to hotel workers that the bed sheets don't require changing. The Healthy Earth Hotel laundry hangers work similarly. These hangers feature two rungs and an explanatory note asking guests to keep clean towels on the top rung, and hang soiled towels on the bottom rung. This way, hotel personnel don't need to wash both the soiled and the clean towels.

The benefits of this safe and simple program are basically boundless. From the perspective of a hotel proprietor, the Healthy Earth Hotel plan is fiscally brilliant—it will save incredible amounts of money and resources. Hotel managers spend literally millions of dollars each year on the electricity, water, detergents, and washing machines needed to do the laundry. Cutting unnecessary financial burdens, such as laundering linens that aren't soiled, can save a bundle. When hotel managers save money, they can afford to offer more reasonable rates to their guests.

Saving money is just one of many reasons hotel owners and guests alike support the Healthy Earth Hotel plan. Another reason is that the program does not involve any unreasonable sacrifice. Not many people wash towels and bed sheets after a single day's use, so why would hotels be expected to? Guests understand this principle, and will appreciate the hotel's sensitivity to environmental concerns.

Looking at a broader perspective, there's an even more positive aspect to this plan. The Healthy Earth Hotel program helps to preserve the planet's precious natural resources. All of the materials and energy that hotels use for their laundering either subtract from the world's resources or cause pollution. Reducing the amount of laundry a hotel does is an automatic benefit to the environment. Many people go on vacations in order to enjoy the splendor of nature, whether it's to the Grand Canyon, a balmy beach, or a sparkling rural lake. Since hotels rely on these travelers, shouldn't they help to keep nature beautiful? The answer is a definitive yes. The Healthy Earth Hotel should be implemented whenever possible.

Questions

1. What was probably the author's purpose in writing this passage?

   A   to inform readers about the Healthy Earth Hotel program
   B   to convince hotels to consider the Healthy Earth Hotel program
   C   to persuade readers that the Healthy Earth Hotel program is a good idea
   D   to offer a comparison of the pros and cons of the Healthy Earth Hotel program

 Tip

Consider the audience. To whom is the author writing?

2. What is the author's opinion of preserving Earth's natural resources?

   F   It's a good idea if it's cost effective.
   G   It's even more important than money.
   H   People should not make or cause pollution.
   J   Hotel guests should take the initiative to save the Earth.

 Tip

Reread the passage. What does the author say in the first sentence of the last paragraph?

3. This passage is an example of—

   A   an autobiography
   B   a persuasive essay
   C   a letter to an editor
   D   an instructional essay

 Tip

Eliminate incorrect answer choices and then choose the best answer.

Check your answers on the next page.

AUTHOR'S PURPOSE   Lesson 4

Passage 2: "Healthy Earth Hotels"

 Answers

1. C   The passage is persuasive. The author is strongly in favor of the Healthy Earth Hotel program. With this in mind, both answer choices B and C might seem correct. However, the author is not writing to hotel owners. He is telling readers—the general public—about the program. Therefore, answer choice C is the best answer.

2. G   In the last paragraph of the essay, the author describes preserving the Earth's resources as an "even more positive aspect of this plan." Prior to this, he discusses money. Therefore, he considers saving the Earth even more important than finances.

3. B   This passage is an essay; it's not a letter or a biography. It also persuades the reader that the Healthy Earth Hotel program is a good idea. Therefore, answer choice B is the best answer.

Passage 3

Read this passage and answer the questions that follow.

Iroquois Dreams

Long before Europeans ventured into what is now the State of New York, native Indians from the Iroquois, Mohawk, Oneida, Onondaga, and Cayuga tribes formed the mighty Iroquois Nation. This group of Indians thrived due to its strong political organization, military power, and sense of unity. Though historians credit several factors for the Iroquois strength, the Iroquois themselves attribute much of their success to their ability to follow their dreams.

The Iroquois use their dreams as a guide to every part of their lives. They rely on their dreams to lead them in everything from marriage to hunting to battle. In fact, in times past, if a tribal member dreamed of failure in battle, the tribe would retreat or postpone their attempt. Throughout their history, dreams were very important to the Iroquois way of life. The Iroquois listen carefully to their dreams and follow their dreams with precision. In fact, the Iroquois feel that to disobey even one dream could bring great misfortune.

There are many examples of how the Iroquois viewed their future through their dreams. Because they wanted to be sure of what their dreams meant, they used the skills of other tribal members who were known as dream interpreters. One historic example is of a mother who dreamed that her unborn son would become a great peacemaker. Her son became a famous Iroquois chief named Ely Parker.

Before his birth, Parker's mother dreamed of seeing a broken rainbow stretching from a white man's home in Buffalo to her reservation in Indian Falls. Disturbed by the dream and confused by its possible meaning, she visited a dream interpreter. The dream interpreter told her that her son would grow up to be a great peacemaker. The interpreter went on to explain that her son would become famous among both the Iroquois and the white man. As it turns out, Parker grew to become a leader for the Union in the Civil War. In the end, he played a significant role in writing the terms of surrender for the Civil War. Parker did indeed become a learned man who was admired by both the white man and the Iroquois.

It's easy to see why the Iroquois put so much effort into accurately understanding their dreams. They felt that dreams could cure disease and lead them to the secret longings of their souls. They also felt that to disobey or ignore dreams would bring about illness and disaster not only for themselves but also for fellow tribal members. The Iroquois would often gather to share their dreams and discuss their interpretations. They also gathered to reenact their dreams, acting out their dreams with other members of the tribe.

These community get-togethers often involved the False Face Society, which consisted of chosen Iroquois who wore carved masks and performed dances. There were several major ceremonies throughout the year where the False Face Society would lead dream interpretations. One of the biggest ceremo-

AUTHOR'S PURPOSE Lesson 4

nies was called the Midwinter Dream Festival, which ends the old year and brings in the new year. The festival centers on thanksgiving for the past and hope for the future. The lessons and healing from past dreams are remembered in song and dance. The mothers and grandmothers of the tribe also take part in a ritual called dreamsharing. They gather to share dreams they felt were helpful and dreams that they felt were confusing and needed further interpretation.

In the Ceremony of the Great Riddle, the Iroquois told their dreams to experts in dream guessing. These experts gave the dreamers hints as to what the dreams really meant. If the dreamer felt that the dream expert was helpful in finding the true meaning of the dream, the dreamer gave a token gift to the interpreter.

The Iroquois also used handmade dreamcatchers to catch their dreams and to protect them from nightmares. Dreamcatchers have become popular decorations for many people today, but the Iroquois as well as other American Indians relied on them to catch their dreams, both good and bad. The beads that were woven into the dreamcatcher were meant to guide good dreams through the center hole of the dreamcatcher web, while the bad dreams would get caught in the web. The good dreams would go through the hole and follow the feathers off the dreamcatcher and into another night's dream.

 Questions

1. What was probably the author's purpose in writing this passage?

    A   to explain that the Iroquois considered dreams important
    B   to entertain readers with a tale about Iroquois dreams
    C   to convince readers to interpret their dreams as the Iroquois did
    D   to describe what it was like to be an Iroquois in what is now New York

 Tip

Think about what most of this passage is about. Then consider the author's purpose.

2. The author probably included the information about Ely Parker to—

    F   describe how powerful some Iroquois leaders were

    (G) emphasize the importance dreams played in Iroquois life

    H   show the role that peace played in the Iroquois way of life

    J   explain that dream interpreters could make someone powerful

Tip

Go back and reread the section of the passage that discusses Ely Parker. Why do you think the author included this information? How does the author introduce this anecdote?

3. You would most likely find this passage in

    A   a newspaper.

    B   a collection of short stories.

    (C) a book about Native Americans.

    D   a magazine article about the Civil War.

Tip

What type of passage is this? Consider what it is mostly about.

Check your answers with those on the next page. Be sure to read the explanation after each answer.

Passage 3: "Iroquois Dreams"

 **Answers**

1. A   The author of this passage does not try to convince the reader, and this passage isn't fiction so its purpose isn't to entertain, so you can eliminate both answer choice B and C. The author does not describe what it was like to be an Iroquois in New York during this time, so you can eliminate answer choice D. Answer choice A is the correct answer.

2. G   The author included the information about Ely Parker to stress the importance of dreams to the Iroquois. Answer choice G is the best answer.

3. C   You would not likely find this passage in a newspaper, since it does not tell about anything recent. It is not fiction, so you would not find it in a collection of short stories. It is not really about the Civil War, so you wouldn't find it in a magazine article about the Civil War. Answer choice C is the best answer to this question.

Passage 4

Now read this passage. Think about the author's purpose as you read. When you finish, answer the questions that follow.

Beating Writer's Block

Imagine a boy sitting at his classroom desk, switching on an electronic word processor, or placing an empty pad of paper in front of him. He has at his disposal the instruments for writing—a pencil, pen, or a computer keyboard—and he is motivated to write, and yet he doesn't . . . or just can't.

The minutes tick by, and the boy stares at the empty paper or screen. He feels puzzled by his inability to organize his words and ideas, and then he becomes frustrated, which makes it even harder to think clearly. He jots down a few words and then, grumbling, erases them. Hours pass and he still hasn't accomplished anything.

Are you familiar with this sort of scenario? If you are, then you've experienced writer's block. This is a frustrating phenomenon that affects many potential writers. It restrains their creativity, keeps their productivity low, and generally makes writing a miserable chore. However, examining this confounding problem and some ways to reduce its effect on you can make writing enjoyable again.

Writer's block may have many easily understood causes, including tiredness or lack of fresh ideas. It may also have more underlying causes, like ugly emotions such as self-doubt. You may feel like you are incapable of writing anything valuable or that you could stare at the paper or screen for months without producing anything worthwhile. You may start to feel that writing is just not worth all the hassle.

Regardless of the cause, writer's block typically carries along feelings of panic, dissatisfaction, frustration, and additional self-doubt. Maybe the scariest thing about writer's block is that it seems to regenerate itself. The more blocked up your words are, the worse you feel about it—the worse you feel about it, the more your words block up!

So, your objective is to discover a method of breaking that gloomy cycle. Initially, you should think about other factors in your life that might be bothering you. These factors may be completely unrelated to writing (like failing a math test or arguing with a friend) that are clouding your thoughts. Working on a remedy to that concern may reduce your writer's block, as well as improve the rest of your daily life.

If the roots of your writer's block are simpler, then the solutions will likely also be simpler. There are dozens of fun, easy ways to kick writer's block out of your schedule!

Here's a scenario you may recognize: you have a writing assignment due early the next morning, but you haven't been able to get a grip on it yet. You're becoming frustrated and anxious as the hours pass but the paper remains empty. The first thing to do is remind yourself that negative feelings like frustration and anxiety are only going to add to your burden. When your brain is relaxed, you can then focus on getting your writing done right.

You've probably heard of "brainstorming," one useful tactic for dealing with writer's block. To brainstorm, just use a separate paper and scribble down whatever ideas come to mind. It may help to start by writing down your topic, and then making a simple diagram to show ideas related to that topic. If your topic was anacondas, you might write "anacondas" and then draw lines that connect concepts like "What they look like," "What they eat," "Where they live," and so on.

If you're capable of choosing or modifying your topic, be sure it's something you're interested in. You probably wouldn't be too enthusiastic about writing an essay on the history of socks! Choose something that excites your mind, because if you're excited about writing, the reader will likely be more excited to read.

Sometimes writer's block occurs because there are too many distractions around that interrupt your concentration. The distractions may be as elementary as a dripping faucet or the sound of voices upstairs, or more complicated, like worries over other obligations you may have. Whatever the distraction, it's not helping your writing. Try to always devote enough time for writing, and avoid noises or activities that can distract you. If you write with undivided attention, you'll likely finish sooner and have more time to focus on other concerns.

If a tight deadline isn't breathing down your neck, your options for beating writer's block are almost endless. Simply think of something that would relax you and clear out your brain. You can work on a separate project, take a walk, play a video game, watch a movie, read a chapter of a good book, or even take a nap. Some of these stress relievers may be just what you need to unclog your writer's block and let the words flow again.

 Questions

1. Which kind of article did the author write about writer's block?

   A   an amusing article that retells true stories about conquering writer's block
   B   a persuasive article that convinces readers that they can conquer writer's block
   C   an informative article that discusses writer's block and how readers can overcome it
   D   a helpful article that teachers readers how to write an essay without experience writer's block

 Tip

Go back and reread the article. What is the author's purpose?

2. The author would probably agree with which statement?

    F   Some people never experience writer's block.
    G   Good planning can help you avoid writer's block.
    H   Overconfidence is a common cause of writer's block.
    J   Stress has little to do with experiencing writer's block

Tip

Reread the passage and eliminate incorrect answer choices. Which answer choice is true based on the information in the passage?

3. This passage would most likely be found in

    A   a magazine for students
    B   a novel for teenagers
    C   a book of short stories
    D   a book about careers

Tip

To correctly answer this question, think about the audience. To whom is the author writing? Is this passage fiction or nonfiction? Choose the answer choice that tells where you would most likely find it.

Check your answers on the next page.

Passage 4: "Beating Writer's Block"

 Answers

1. C   The article is informative. It tells about writer's block and offers some suggestions for over-coming it. Answer choice C is the best answer.

2. G   The author says that writer's block can occur when you put off doing a writing assignment and it is due the next morning. Therefore, the author seems to believe that good planning might help you overcome writer's block. Answer choice G is the best answer.

3. A   The author is writing to students and the passage is informative. Therefore, answer choice A is the best answer.

# Lesson 5: Literature

New York State Learning Standard:

S2 Literary Response and Expression

Subskills:

Interpret theme (S2)

Interpret characters (S2)

Interpret plot (S2)

Determine use of literary device (S2)

Questions about literature

Literary passages are fiction. For the New York State test, they may be short stories, poems, or excerpts from novels. They might ask about the **theme** of literature. Remember that the theme is the message that an author is trying to convey in his or her work. Questions on this test might often ask you about **characters** and their motivations, why characters in stories do the things that they do. Some questions will ask you about the **plot**, what happens in a piece of writing and how problems are resolved.

Questions that ask you to **determine the use of literary devices** will often give you answer options and ask you to identify the one that is an example of personification or a metaphor or simile. You might be asked about the rhyme scheme of a poem and about the point of view, whether an author uses first, second, or third person.

 Activity

Read the following fable. Then write a brief character sketch of the fox. Consider what he is like and why he acts the way that he does.

The Fox and the Stork
(adapted from Aesop's Fables)

Once upon a time, the fox and the stork were friends. The fox invited the stork to dinner. He loved soup, so he placed soup in two shallow bowls on the table. The fox ate his soup, but the stork could not eat hers. She tried and tried, but could not get the soup out of the shallow bowl with her long, pointed beak. The stork tried to be polite to the fox, though, just in case he did not realize his error. The stork was very hungry, however, and eventually became angry. "I'm sorry the soup is not to your liking," the fox said.

"Oh, do not apologize," said the stork. "I hope you will return this visit and dine with me soon."

So the two chose a day and the fox visited the stork for dinner. The stork also served delicious soup, but in a very long-necked jar with a narrow mouth. The fox could not get the soup out of the jar. "I will not apologize for dinner," said the stork. "One bad turn deserves another."

_____

_____

_____

_____

Activity

Read the following fable. Then write a brief character sketch of the goat. Consider what he is like and where he went wrong.

The Fox and the Goat
(adapted from Aesop's Fables)

One day a fox fell deep into a well while trying to get a drink of water and could not get out again. He waited there until a thirsty goat came along to get a drink as well. The goat saw the fox at the bottom of the well and asked him how the water tasted.

"Oh, sir goat, this is the best water I've ever had!" shouted the Fox excitedly. "You simply must taste this water. You look very thirsty."

The goat grinned and nodded his head. He jumped down into the well, landing next to the fox, and started to drink. Now both animals were trapped in the well.

"How will we get out?" asked the goat nervously, for he was beginning to worry.

"If you put your feet on the wall and stretch up as far as you can," said the fox, "I'll climb up your back and then pull you out when I am at the top." The goat agreed, but once the fox was out, he kept running.

"Come back here!" cried the angry goat. "You broke your promise!"

"Yes, but you were foolish!" called the fox. "If you had not been thinking only about your thirst, you never would have been trapped to begin with. You should learn now to look before you leap!"

Passage 1

As you read the following passage, think about the narrator. What kind of person is she? When you finish reading, answer the questions that follow.

Excerpt from *Bleak House* (Chapter 3) by Charles Dickens

I have a great deal of difficulty in beginning to write my portion of these pages, for I know I am not clever. I always knew that. I can remember, when I was a very little girl indeed, I used to say to my doll, when we were alone together, "Now Dolly, I am not clever, you know very well, and you must be patient with me, like a dear!" And so she used to sit propped up in a great arm-chair, with her beautiful complexion and rosy lips, staring at me—or not so much at me, I think, as at nothing—while I busily stitched away, and told her every one of my secrets.

My dear old doll! I was such a little shy thing that I seldom dared to open my lips, and never dared to open my heart, to anybody else. It almost makes me cry to think what a relief it used to be to me, when I came home from school of a day, to turn up-stairs to my room, and say, "O you dear faithful Dolly, I knew you would be expecting me!" and then to sit down on the floor, leaning on the elbow of her great chair, and tell her all I had noticed since we parted. I had always rather a noticing way—not a quick way, O no!—a silent way of noticing what passed before me, and thinking I should like to understand it better. I have not by any means a quick understanding. When I love a person very tenderly indeed, it seems to brighten. But even that may be my vanity.

 Questions

1. Why did the narrator talk to her doll?

   The narrator talked to her doll because she is shy to talk to other people, only the doll is her friend.

2. How does the narrator feel about her doll?

   The narrator loves her doll, the doll is her only friend. She only dared to talk to the doll, because she is shy

3. Why do you think the narrator doesn't like talking to other people?

I think the narrator doesn't like talking to other people she thought she isn't clever.

Check your answers on the next page.

Passage 1: "Excerpt from *Bleak House*"

 Answers

1. **Sample answer:** The narrator talked to her doll because she was shy and did not feel comfortable talking to other people. In school she was quiet and noticed things that she wanted to tell to someone, but she was afraid to open up to other people. When she got home, she told these things to her doll instead, and this made her feel better.

2. **Sample answer:** The narrator loves her doll and said it was a great relief to come home to it each day.

3. **Sample answer:** The narrator seems unsure of herself and has no confidence. As a girl, she was quiet because she was probably afraid that her peers would judge her negatively based on her stories and ideas. She tells the reader negative things about herself—she says she is not clever, she does not have a quick understanding, and she is vain—before the reader can make a negative judgment about her.

Passage 2

Read the following poem and answer the questions that follow. As you read, think about the message the author is trying to convey.

Up-Hill
by Christina Rossetti

Does the road wind up-hill all the way?
   Yes, to the very end.
Will the day's journey take the whole long day?
   From morn to night, my friend.

But is there for the night a resting-place?
   A roof for when the slow dark hours begin.
May not the darkness hide it from my face?
   You cannot miss that inn.

Shall I meet other wayfarers at night?
   Those who have gone before.
Then must I knock, or call when just in sight?
   They will not keep you standing at that door.

Shall I find comfort, travel-sore and weak?
   Of labour you shall find the sum.
Will there be beds for me and all who seek?
   Yea, beds for all who come.

 Questions

1. How does the author feel about setting out on this journey?

    (A) curious 好奇的
    B excited
    C regretful 后悔的
    D miserable

 Tip

Reread the poem and consider the speaker's tone. What has the speaker done to let us know how she feels?

2. What will happen when the author reaches the inn?

    F She must knock on the door.
    (G) She will be greeted and invited in to sleep.
    H She will have to wait until morning for a bed.
    J She must call out when she is close to the inn.

 Tip

Reread the third stanza of the poem.

3. Why do you think that all those who have come before are still at the inn? What does this say about the inn? Use details from the poem in your answer.

    I think that all those who have come before are still at the inn is because they thought the inn is good. That tells us the inn is a good place to rest. The bed in the inn are comfortable and all people who come will have a bed.

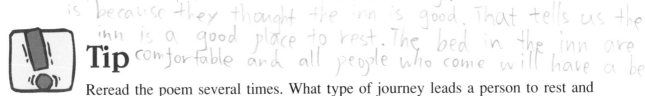 **Tip**

Reread the poem several times. What type of journey leads a person to rest and never leave? What might the inn represent?

Check your answers on the next page.

Passage 2: "Up-Hill"

 Answers

1. A   The speaker's questions reveal that she is curious, but consider the other answer choices before choosing this answer. The speaker has done nothing to suggest that she is excited, and she does not seem regretful or miserable about the journey. The correct answer is A.

2. G   The speaker asks if she should knock or call out and is told that she will not be kept waiting at the door, meaning that neither action is necessary. Because she is told that she will not have to wait, answer choice H is incorrect. You can conclude that answer choice G is correct.

3.   **Sample answer:** All those who have come before are still at the inn because it represents a final resting place or destination. The author's journey is not an actual trip but a search for comfort from feeling "travel-sore and weak," or a rest after a long and hard life.

Passage 3

Read this passage and answer the questions that follow.

Excerpt from *Incidents in the Life of a Slave Girl*
by Harriet Jacobs

A small shed had been added to my grandmother's house years ago. Some boards were laid across the joists at the top, and between these boards and the roof was a very small garret, never occupied by anything but rats and mice. It was a pent roof, covered with nothing but shingles, according to the southern custom for such buildings. The garret was only nine feet long and seven wide. The highest part was three feet high, and sloped down abruptly to the loose board floor. There was no admission for either light or air. My uncle Phillip, who was a carpenter, had very skillfully made a concealed trap-door, which communicated with the storeroom. He had been doing this while I was waiting in the swamp. The storeroom opened upon a piazza. To this hole I was conveyed as soon as I entered the house. The air was stifling; the darkness total. A bed had been spread on the floor. I could sleep quite comfortably on one side; but the slope was so sudden that I could not turn on the other without hitting the roof. The rats and mice ran over my bed; but I was weary, and I slept such sleep as the wretched may, when a tempest has passed over them. Morning came. I knew it only by the noises I heard; for in my small den day and night were all the same. I suffered for air even more than for light. But I was not comfortless. I heard the voices of my children. There was joy and there was sadness in the sound. It made my tears flow. How I longed to speak to them! I was eager to look on their faces; but there was no hole, no crack, through which I could peep. This continued darkness was oppressive. It seemed horrible to sit or lie in a cramped position day after day, without one gleam of light. Yet I would have chosen this, rather than my lot as a slave, though white people considered it an easy one; and it was so compared with the fate of others. I was never cruelly overworked; I was never lacerated with the whip from head to foot; I was never so beaten and bruised that I could not turn from one side to the other; I never had my heel-strings cut to prevent my running away; I was never chained to a log and forced to drag it about, while I toiled in the fields from morning till night; I was never branded with hot iron, or torn by bloodhounds. On the contrary, I had always been kindly treated, and tenderly cared for, until I came into the hands of Dr. Flint. I had never wished for freedom until then. But though my life in slavery was comparatively devoid of hardships, God pity the woman who is compelled to lead such a life!

My food was passed up to me through the trap-door my uncle had contrived; and my grandmother, my uncle Phillip, and aunt Nancy would seize such opportunities as they could, to mount up there and chat with me at the opening. But of course this was not safe in the daytime. It must all be done in darkness. It was impossible for me to move in an erect position, but I crawled about my den for exercise. One day I hit my head against something, and found it was a gimlet. My uncle had left it sticking there when he made the trap-door. I was as rejoiced as Robinson Crusoe could have been at finding such a treasure. It put a lucky thought into my head. I said to myself, "Now I will have some light. Now I will see my children." I did not dare to begin my work during the daytime, for fear of attracting attention. But I grouped round; and having found the side next the street, where I could frequently see my children, I stuck the gimlet in and waited for the evening. I bored three rows of holes, one above another; then I bored out the interstices between. I thus succeeded in making one hole about an inch long and an inch broad. I sat by it till late into the night, to enjoy the little whiff of air that floated in. In the morning

I watched for my children. The first person I saw in the street was Dr. Flint. I had a shuddering, superstitious feeling that it was a bad omen. Several familiar faces passed by. At last I heard the merry laugh of children, and presently two sweet little faces were looking up at me, as though they knew I was there, and were conscious of the joy they imparted. How I longed to *tell* them I was there!

 Questions

1. Who has locked up the narrator?

    A   her children
    B   Dr. Flint
    C   her uncle Phillip
    D   her master

 Tip

This question asks you about the plot of the story. Remember that the narrator says she is no longer a slave.

2. What might happen if the narrator is discovered?

    F   She won't leave her hiding place.
    G   She might scare her grandmother.
    H   She won't be able to see her children.
    J   She might be forced back into slavery.

 Tip

Consider why the author is hiding in the first place. What might happen if people find out that she is hiding there?

3.   What is the narrator's biggest problem in the story?

   A   She hates being in the dark.
   B   She is afraid of rats and mice.
   C   She wants to see her children.
   D   She wants to talk to her grandmother.

 # Tip

This question asks you about the plot of the story. What does the narrator do at the end of the story? Why does she do this?

Check your answers on the next page.

Passage 3: "Excerpt from *Incidents in the Life of a Slave Girl*"

 Answers

1. B   The narrator says that Dr. Flint has locked her up. Answer choice B is the correct answer.

2. J   The author is hiding because she is an escaped slave. If she is discovered, she might have to return to her life as a slave. The correct answer is J.

3. C   Though the narrator complains about the dark, she says that the lack of air is worse. Throughout the passage, the narrator repeatedly wishes to see her children. Answer choice C is correct.

Passage 4

Read the following story. Think about Seth's problem as you read and how his outlook changes throughout the story. Then answer the questions that follow.

Mr. Salazar

Wearing new shorts and a new shirt and with his book bag on his back, Seth headed for the bus stop. *The first day of school is always a blast,* Seth thought. He couldn't wait to see some of his friends that he wasn't able to see over summer vacation while he worked with his grandfather on his peach farm.

Seth was certain that eighth grade was going to be his best year ever. As one of the oldest students, he knew just about everyone in the school. He was going to be on the varsity basketball team and might even be chosen as a starter. The best part was having Mr. Jordan as his homeroom teacher. Mr. Jordan had been Seth's English teacher for several years and Seth really enjoyed his classes, mainly because Mr. Jordan had a great sense of humor. He loved to laugh and he made learning new material great fun. After the class had read a new short story or novel, he would match students to characters and have them act out a chapter or two. While at first Seth thought this would be extremely corny and considered outright refusing to do it, he changed his mind when Mr. Jordan assigned him the part of an old woman in one of Flannery O'Connor's short stories. Seth tried in vain to raise his deep voice so it sounded like a woman's, but all he managed to do was squeak. The class was hysterical. Then Mr. Jordan assigned Seth's friend Charlie the part of a desk! Once everyone had their parts, they managed to get through it without laughing too loudly. Mr. Jordan discussed character motivation by asking each student (except Charlie) what made their character do the things that he or she did. Mr. Jordan was Seth's all-time favorite teacher.

That's why Seth was completely distraught to see another man standing in front of Mr. Jordan's desk. "Who's *that*?" he asked his friend Ashley. "And why is he in Mr. Jordan's classroom?" Ashley shook her head and told Seth she had no clue. The man was much younger than Mr. Jordan and, even though he hunched his shoulders and leaned forward slightly, he was extremely tall—too tall in Seth's opinion. The man slipped his hands into his pockets nervously and smiled an awkward, crooked smile. When Seth's eyes met his, he nodded, but Seth was too bewildered to respond.

When everyone entered the room the man introduced himself as Mr. Salazar. "Are you a substitute?" called out someone from the back of class.

"Nope. I'm going to be your teacher this year. Mr. Jordan and his wife relocated to New Jersey about a month ago. I was hired to take his place—and I'm honored to be your teacher this year."

Seth could not believe his ears. No more Mr. Jordan? That meant no more funny plays, no joking around in class—no more fun. This man looked serious, nervous, and too young to be a teacher. "Is this the first class you've ever taught?" Seth inquired.

Mr. Salazar laughed. "Yes," he replied. "I graduated college last May, but I student-taught during my last year. I'm going to teach you many new and interesting things and we're going to have lots of fun learning."

Yeah right, Seth thought. *This is going to ruin everything.*

Seth and his friend Charlie made a beeline for the basketball court at recess. Seth was surprised to see Mr. Salazar on the court dribbling a basketball. His lanky frame moved surprisingly swiftly as he approached the hoop. He reached up and gently shot the ball—swish! Mr. Salazar stopped when he saw them. "Hey, boys. Would you like to play?" he asked.

Seth and Charlie approached him. Two other boys walked onto the court. "*You* play basketball?" Seth asked.

"You bet!" replied Mr. Salazar. "I played in both high school and college."

Seth caught the rebound and tried unsuccessfully to pass by Mr. Salazar. Seth laughed. "For a too-tall teacher, you can really move," he said. Mr. Salazar knocked the ball away from Seth and sunk it in the hoop. A crowd of students gathered around the court to watch Mr. Salazar play. The boys tried to beat him four to one, but it was no use. Exhausted, Seth plopped down on the side of the court. "You're so tall no one can beat you," Seth said.

"Nah," Mr. Salazar replied and sunk yet another basket. "Size doesn't have all that much to do with it. Some of the best players on my college team were only average height if not smaller. It's how you move that counts."

"Well, you sure can move," Seth said. "Could you teach us to move like that?"

"Sure!" said Mr. Salazar. "I'm going to teach you lots of things—and not just about basketball. We're going to start a new novel in English today. It's called *Dogsong*. Have you ever heard of it?"

Dogsong was written by Gary Paulsen, Seth's favorite author. Seth told Mr. Salazar about the other books he had read by Paulsen. When the bell rang ending recess, Seth headed back to class excitedly for the first time since he arrived at school. Maybe things weren't so bad after all.

 **Questions**

1. What does Seth think will be the best part of going back to school?

    A   He will be one of the oldest students.
    B   Mr. Jordan will be his homeroom teacher.
    C   He will be on the varsity basketball team.
    D   All of his friends will be back from summer vacation.

 Tip

Reread the first paragraph of the story. What is the main reason Seth is excited to go back to school?

2. What literary device does Seth use when he refers to Mr. Salazar as a "too-tall teacher"?

   F simile 明口前
   G paradox 和 6
   H metaphor 比り前
   J alliteration 羊文

Tip

Read this phrase to yourself. What about this phrase suggests that a literary device is being used?

3. Which pair of words best describes Mr. Salazar?

   A serious but nice
   B nervous but tricky
   C inexperienced but kind
   D unsure but persistent

Tip

Eliminate the incorrect answer choices and then choose the one that best describes Mr. Salazar.

4. How does Seth's character change throughout the story? Support your answer with details and information from the story.

Tip

Reread the story. Note Seth's feelings as the story progresses.

Check your answers on the next page.

Passage 4: "Mr. Salazar"

 Answers

1. B In the beginning of the story, Seth thinks that the best part about going back to school will be having Mr. Jordan as a homeroom teacher. The correct answer is B.

2. J Simile, paradox, and metaphor are all literary devices that use comparison. Since nothing is compared in this statement, you can guess that alliteration is the right answer, even if you don't know that it is a device using the repetition of consonant sounds. The correct answer is J.

3. C Mr. Salazar confesses that this is his first teaching job, so he is inexperienced. He seems very kind, however, and willing to try. Answer choice C is correct.

4. **Sample answer:** Seth starts out very excited about the start of the school year because he will have his favorite teacher, Mr. Jordan, as homeroom teacher. He is shocked to discover another man standing in front of Mr. Jordan's desk when he arrives at school. When he learns that this man is taking Mr. Jordan's place, he does not think much of him. He is young and awkward and Seth does not think he will be any good. Seth gets to know the new teacher better when he plays basketball with him, however, and his skill impresses Seth. Then he tells Seth they are going to read a book by Gary Paulsen, Seth's favorite author. Seth's mood improves a bit and seems to be willing to give Mr. Salazar a chance.

Lesson 6: Conclusions and Inferences

New York State Learning Standard:

S1 Information and Understanding

Subskill:

Draw conclusions and make inferences (S1)

What are conclusions and inferences?

When you draw a **conclusion** or make an **inference**, you draw personal meaning from a passage. These types of questions are not stated in the passage, so you won't be able to put your finger on them. You have to determine the answer based on what you have read. In other words, you have to think carefully about what you have read.

When you draw a conclusion, you make a judgment or form an opinion. When you make an inference, you often predict something that will happen based on the facts at hand. You might surmise or guess something about a person, idea, or thing. For example, suppose you are a reading a mystery novel. You are about halfway through it when you conclude that the maid did it, but you also infer that she is crafty and will try to frame the butler.

On the New York State test, questions asking you to draw a conclusion or make an inference often begin with "why" and/or include the words "probably" or "it is likely that."

 **Activity**

Look at the picture above. Draw a conclusion about the two men. Make an inference about what they will do next. Share your conclusion and prediction with the class.

_____

_____

_____

_____

_____

_____

Passage 1

Now read this passage and then answer the questions that follow.

The Truth about Organ Donation

Myths about organ donation have circulated for decades, but most are simply stories invented by people who don't understand the process of organ donation. The truth is that the organs donated from one person's body can save multiple lives. The heart, kidneys, pancreas, lungs, and intestines all can be donated. In addition, eyes and body tissues, such as skin and bone marrow, can be donated. In the United States alone, over 87,000 people are on a waiting list to receive an organ, and these people may wait days, weeks, months, or even years, to receive an organ transplant. It is estimated that about ten to fourteen thousand people who die each year meet the requirements to be organ donors, but only about half of those people actually become organ donors. It is essential that you understand the facts about organ donation, so you can make the right choice when the time comes.

It might not be pleasant to think about what happens to a person's body after he or she passes away, but organ donors know that their organs will be used to save human lives. Many organ donors are victims of accidents or other unexpected traumas, and their organs are perfectly healthy when they arrive in the emergency room. Emergency room doctors work hard to save patients' lives, but sometimes the brain has been so severely damaged that it will never work again. If the brain shows no signs of activity and has no blood supply, doctors consider the brain dead, and the patient becomes a candidate for organ donation.

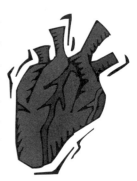

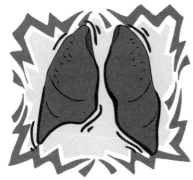

When a patient's family consents to donate the organs to someone in need, the patient is called a "donor." Doctors enter the organ donor's height, weight, and blood type into a computer, which searches for potential matches. The Organ Procurement and Transplantation Network maintains a list of people in need of organs. When a match is found, the patient who will receive the organ is prepared for the transplant surgery. A special team of physicians removes the necessary organs from the organ donor's body. Organs don't last very long outside the body, so once they have been removed they are quickly transported to the hospital where another surgical team is prepared to operate on the organ recipient. In some cases, the patient is ready to leave the hospital just a few days after the transplant surgery, but other times it takes longer for the patient to recover. Either way, most patients can eventually return to their normal lives, and live for many long, healthy years—all because a stranger was selfless enough to donate his or her organs to help save a life.

Becoming an organ donor is relatively easy; anyone, from a newborn baby to a great-great-grandmother, can become an organ donor. In many states, you can declare your organ donor status when you receive or renew your driver's license. You can also complete and carry an organ donor card in your wallet. If you choose to become an organ donor, you should talk to your family about your decision, and make them aware that if something happens to you, you want to donate your organs. Remember, when you make the decision to become an organ donor, you make the decision to save a life.

Questions

1. Why do you think only half of the people eligible to donate organs actually donate them?

   I think only half of the people eligible to donate organs actually donate them is because the donor need to find a match to donate. To find a match, you must have the same height, weight, and blood type.

2. Why is it a good idea to inform your family if you decide to become an organ donor?

   Inform your family if you decide to become an organ donor is a good idea because your decision will make them aware that if something happens to you, and it's an honor to donate you organ, because it's saving a life.

3. Do you think more people will donate organs in the future?

___I think more people will donate organs
in the future because there are more and
more people will realize the organs
can save lives and they will sign up
to donate their organs.___

Check your answers on the next page.

Passage 1: "The Truth about Organ Donation"

 Answers

1. **Sample answer:** The reason that only half of those eligible to donate organs actually do so is that people do not like to think about their own death or giving their organs away. Many people are probably squeamish about this, and do not sign up to be organ donors. They may not realize the importance of the situation.

2. **Sample answer:** Your family might try to interfere if they do not realize that you would like your organs donated. Telling them of your intentions before the unthinkable happens will ensure that your organs go to someone in need.

3. **Sample answer:** I think more people will become organ donors in the future. As more and more people receive organ transplants and live longer than ever before, people will begin to realize that donating their organs is important and can save someone's life.

Passage 2

Now read this excerpt and then answer the questions that follow.

Excerpt from *Hard Times*
by Charles Dickens
CHAPTER I—THE ONE THING NEEDFUL

'NOW, what I want is, Facts. Teach these boys and girls nothing but Facts. Facts alone are wanted in life. Plant nothing else, and root out everything else. You can only form the minds of reasoning animals upon Facts: nothing else will ever be of any service to them. This is the principle on which I bring up my own children, and this is the principle on which I bring up these children. Stick to Facts, sir!'

The scene was a plain, bare, monotonous vault of a school-room, and the speaker's square fore-finger emphasized his observations by underscoring every sentence with a line on the schoolmaster's sleeve. The emphasis was helped by the speaker's square wall of a forehead, which had his eyebrows for its base, while his eyes found commodious cellarage in two dark caves, overshadowed by the wall. The emphasis was helped by the speaker's mouth, which was wide, thin, and hard set. The emphasis was helped by the speaker's voice, which was inflexible, dry, and dictatorial. The emphasis was helped by the speaker's hair, which bristled on the skirts of his bald head, a plantation of firs to keep the wind from its shining surface, all covered with knobs, like the crust of a plum pie, as if the head had scarcely warehouse-room for the hard facts stored inside. The speaker's obstinate carriage, square coat, square legs, square shoulders,—nay, his very neckcloth, trained to take him by the throat with an unaccom-modating grasp, like a stubborn fact, as it was,—all helped the emphasis. 'In this life, we want nothing but Facts, sir; nothing but Facts!'

The speaker, and the schoolmaster, and the third grown person present, all backed a little, and swept with their eyes the inclined plane of little vessels then and there arranged in order, ready to have imperial gallons of facts poured into them until they were full to the brim.

Questions

1. What can you conclude about the speaker's appearance?

    A   He is very old.
    B   He is not neat.
    C   He is very strong.
    D   He is not handsome.

 Tip

Reread the description of the speaker's appearance. What image do you think the author is trying to create?

2. Why does the speaker repeat the word "facts"?

    F   to stress his point
    G   to scare the students
    H   to clear up any confusion
    J   to give the students information

 Tip

Reread the first paragraph of the excerpt.

3. It is likely that the speaker is

    A   the students' teacher.
    B   someone of high authority.
    C   a parent of one of the students.
    D   a friend of the schoolmaster.

 Tip

Reread the beginning and ending of the excerpt.

Check your answers on the next page.

CONCLUSIONS AND INFERENCES   Lesson 6

Passage 2: "Excerpt from *Hard Times*"

 Answers

1.   D   While answer choice C might also seem correct, we know that the speaker seems intimidating, but we really don't know if he is strong. The description of the speaker is definitely not "handsome." Answer choice D is the best answer.

2.   F   Answer choice F is the best answer choice. The speaker is trying to stress the importance of the children learning "facts."

3.   B   The speaker is not the students' teacher, since he tells someone to teach them facts in the beginning of the excerpt, so answer choice A is not the correct answer. He does not seem to be a parent, and we do not know if he is a friend of the schoolmaster. Answer choice B is the best answer.

Passage 3

Now read this excerpt and then answer the questions that follow.

Space Colonization: Too Big a Risk

Just a few decades ago, the idea of establishing colonies in space was viewed as nothing more than a wild science fiction tale. However, as technological advances and scientific discoveries teach us more about the places beyond our planet, space colonization looks increasingly possible. Within our lifetimes, we may see people making an effort to build a permanent city on another planet or even on an asteroid. Perhaps you or I will even travel to the stars for a vacation!

If you were able to vote today on whether or not another planet—the red planet Mars, for instance—should be colonized, would you vote "yes" or "no"? Many people are enthusiastic about this idea and see it as an entirely positive opportunity for the people of Earth. These supporters of space colonization have many good ideas, but may be overlooking some other important information. Colonizing another planet would be one of the biggest steps ever taken in human history. An accomplishment that important carries along many dangers, expenses, and other concerns. Before you make your decision, you should be aware of the possible negative aspects of such an event.

First of all, the complications of establishing a livable city on another planet are staggering. Even the world's finest scientists are still baffled by the question of how they could keep people safe and healthy on the surface of an alien world. People require very special conditions in order to live, and it would be hard to ensure those conditions on an unexplored new world.

Of all the planets, Mars seems like it would best support human visitors—but it's still an inhospitable place. The atmosphere is so thin that it would be impossible to breathe. People would need special equipment in order to get the air they need to live. It's possible that the first colonists would have to spend their entire lives wearing space suits. Also, temperatures on the red planet can become extremely cold—much colder than Antarctica. It might be possible for people to live in such temperatures, but few would find them comfortable!

Although there may have once been flowing water on Mars, today it is a very dry planet. Humans rely on water to live, and colonists would have to bring a large amount of it with them. Special machines would have to be developed in order to recycle the drinking water. Even if the water problem was solved, how would the colonists get food? The Martian ground is rocky and dry; it seems unlikely that any kind of Earth crops could possibly grow there. Until that was figured out, rockets would have to be constantly sent to the colony with fresh supplies; the cost of doing this would be huge.

CONCLUSIONS AND INFERENCES   Lesson 6

Additionally, the overall cost of a colonization mission would be downright breathtaking. Scientists have estimated the price tag of a single mission to be set at about $30 billion. That funding is desperately needed for projects here on our planet. Social programs of all sorts could benefit greatly from even a fraction of that amount. We humans would be wise to invest more time, money, and effort in improving our own world before we start visiting others.

That idea leads into one of the saddest but most important questions we must keep in mind during this age of amazing new technologies: can humans be trusted with a brand new planet? Humans have proven to be very imperfect guests, to say the least. The greatest threats to our current planet are posed by us, its inhabitants. Through weapons, warfare, pollution, and greed, humanity has taken advantage of the natural splendor that Earth once possessed. Some scientists believe that humans have a duty to spread out across the solar system and spread beauty and intelligence. However, over the centuries humans have spread just as much hatred and horror as they've spread beauty and intelligence.

Some supporters of space colonization believe that the nations of Earth would unify and work together to achieve this common goal. These supporters think that all aspects of Earth life, from education to economics, would be improved by the race to colonize space. However, a short survey of history points to opposite ideas.

History shows that colonization has caused greed, hatred, prejudice, and war among the nations of Earth. Imagine the effects of space colonization! Nations would likely struggle to be first to reach the red planet; then they would struggle for the rights to build on the best land; then they would struggle for resources for their colonists. The results could be more mistrust, fear, and conflict. A Mars colony might end up further dividing the people of Earth and yielding more suffering than discovery.

Should a colonization project proceed despite these many problems, what sort of benefits would it bring to the people of Earth? Some scientists have suggested that we build mines in space, to gather valuable metals like iron and gold from asteroids and other celestial bodies. This would return some of the costs of the mission. However, our planet is already well equipped with dozens of types of metal and minerals. In fact, with Earth's natural resources as well as our recycling programs, we have more than enough already. Besides, if we were to build colonies just to make money, greedy competition would no doubt arise that would endanger the whole project.

Some scientists have proclaimed that colonizing the red planet would ensure the survival of the human race. Their argument is that, even if Earth were to die or be destroyed, a group of humans would still exist in their Martian colony. This argument may be true, but it's not a strong argument because it doesn't apply to our world's current situation. Earth is still a healthy and vital planet and promises to remain that way for a very long time. The human race is growing every year and is definitely not endangered. We humans can live on for millions of years longer on Earth, if only we learn to behave more responsibly.

In conclusion, the concept of space colonization is a fascinating one, but it is fraught with problems and dangers. There may be a time when humans are ready to build their cities on the surface of Mars. However, attempting to conquer Mars now, while neglecting Earth, might bring enormous damage to Earth and its inhabitants.

Questions

1. What is probably the main reason some people would like to live in space?

   A   to escape from conflict
   B   to learn more about Earth
   C   to prove that it can be done
   D   to profit from the experience

 Tip

Reread the beginning of the passage. What do you think is the main reason some people would like to be part of a space colony?

2. What is the author's strongest reason against space colonization?

   F   fear
   G   cost
   H   danger
   J   conflict

 Tip

Reread the passage and choose the answer choice that seems to be his most important reason.

3. Why do you think the author believes that the human race will survive on Earth for many more years to come?

   (A) The population is increasing.
   B   Technology is advancing quickly.
   C   Medical advances are being made.
   D   Conflict among nations has been reduced.

Tip

Reread the end of the passage. Consider why the author thinks the future of the human race is not in danger on Earth.

4. Do you think a space colony will be established during the next few decades? Why or why not?

   No, I don't thing a space colony will be established during the next few decades, because as the author said, the colonization will be dangerous and expensive

Check your answers on the next page.

Passage 3: "Space Colonization: Too Big a Risk"

 Answers

1. C   The passage implies that people would like to live in space to prove it can be done. If you were unsure of this answer, you could have chosen it simply by process of elimination. The other answer choices are not implied in the passage.

2. G   While the author indicates that establishing a space colony is dangerous, the main reason he is against it is cost. Answer choice G is the best answer.

3. A   If you reread the end of the article, you can conclude that the author believes the human race will continue to exist on Earth because the population is increasing.

4.   **Sample answer:** While we might be able to establish a space colony, I don't think this will happen during our lifetime. As the author states, it simply costs too much money. We need to take care of everyone on our planet first. I think the American public would be strongly against spending this much money to establish a space colony.

Passage 4

Excerpt from *The Secret Garden*
by Frances Hodgson Burnett
from Chapter 15 – "Nest Building"

In her talks with Colin, Mary had tried to be very cautious about the secret garden. There were certain things she wanted to find out from him, but she felt that she must find them out without asking him direct questions. In the first place, as she began to like to be with him, she wanted to discover whether he was the kind of boy you could tell a secret to. He was not in the least like Dickon, but he was evidently so pleased with the idea of a garden no one knew anything about that she thought perhaps he could be trusted. But she had not known him long enough to be sure. The second thing she wanted to find out was this: If he could be trusted–if he really could–wouldn't it be possible to take him to the garden without having any one find it out? The grand doctor had said that he must have fresh air and Colin had said that he would not mind fresh air in a secret garden. Perhaps if he had a great deal of fresh air and knew Dickon and the robin and saw things growing he might not think so much about dying. Mary had seen herself in the glass sometimes lately when she had realized that she looked quite a different creature from the child she had seen when she arrived from India. This child looked nicer. Even Martha had seen a change in her.

On that first morning when the sky was blue again, Mary wakened very early. The sun was pouring in slanting rays through the blinds and there was something so joyous in the sight of it that she jumped out of bed and ran to the window. She drew up the blinds and opened the window itself and a great waft of fresh, scented air blew in upon her. The moor was blue and the whole world looked as if something Magic had happened to it. There were tender little fluting sounds here and there and everywhere, as if scores of birds were beginning to tune up for a concert. Mary put her hand out of the window and held it in the sun.

"It's warm–warm!" she said. "It will make the green points push up and up and up, and it will make the bulbs and roots work and struggle with all their might under the earth."

She kneeled down and leaned out of the window as far as she could, breathing big breaths and sniffing the air until she laughed because she remembered what Dickon's mother had said about the end of his nose quivering like a rabbit's. "It must be very early," she said. "The little clouds are all pink and I've never seen the sky look like this. No one is up. I don't even hear the stable boys."

A sudden thought made her scramble to her feet.

"I can't wait! I am going to see the garden!" . . .

When she had reached the place where the door hid itself under the ivy, she was startled by a curious loud sound. It was the caw–caw of a crow and it came from the top of the wall, and when she looked up, there sat a big glossy-plumaged blue-black bird, looking down at her very wisely indeed. She had never seen a crow so close before and he made her a little nervous, but the next moment he spread his wings and flapped away across the garden. She hoped he was not going to stay inside and she pushed the door open wondering if he would. When she got fairly into the garden she saw that he probably did intend to stay because he had alighted on a dwarf apple-tree and under the apple-tree was lying a little reddish animal with a Bushy tail, and both of them were watching the stooping body and rust-red head of Dickon, who was kneeling on the grass working hard.

Mary flew across the grass to him.

"Oh, Dickon! Dickon!" she cried out. "How could you get here so early! How could you! The sun has only just got up!"

He got up himself, laughing and glowing, and tousled; his eyes like a bit of the sky.

"Eh!" he said. "I was up long before him. How could I have stayed abed! Th' world's all fair begun again this mornin', it has. An' it's workin' an' hummin' an' scratchin' an' pipin' an' nest-buildin' an' breathin' out scents, till you've got to be out on it 'stead o' lyin' on your back. When th' sun did jump up, th' moor went mad for joy, an' I was in the midst of th' heather, an' I run like mad myself, shoutin' an' singin'. An' I come straight here. I couldn't have stayed away. Why, th' garden was lyin' here waitin'!"

Mary put her hands on her chest, panting, as if she had been running herself.

"Oh, Dickon! Dickon!" she said. "I'm so happy I can scarcely breathe!"

Seeing him talking to a stranger, the little bushy-tailed animal rose from its place under the tree and came to him, and the rook, cawing once, flew down from its branch and settled quietly on his shoulder.

"This is th' little fox cub," he said, rubbing the little reddish animal's head. "It's named Captain. An' this here's Soot. Soot he flew across th' moor with me an' Captain he run same as if th' hounds had been after him. They both felt same as I did."

Neither of the creatures looked as if he were the least afraid of Mary. When Dickon began to walk about, Soot stayed on his shoulder and Captain trotted quietly close to his side.

"See here!" said Dickon. "See how these has pushed up, an' these an' these! An' Eh! Look at these here!"

CONCLUSIONS AND INFERENCES Lesson 6

He threw himself upon his knees and Mary went down beside him. They had come upon a whole clump of crocuses burst into purple and orange and gold. Mary bent her face down and kissed and kissed them. . . . There was every joy on earth in the secret garden that morning, and in the midst of them came a delight more delightful than all, because it was more wonderful. Swiftly something flew across the wall and darted through the trees to a close grown corner, a little flare of red-breasted bird with something hanging from its beak. Dickon stood quite still and put his hand on Mary almost as if they had suddenly found themselves laughing in a church.

"We munnot stir," he whispered in broad Yorkshire. "We munnot scarce breathe. I knowed he was mate-huntin' when I seed him last. It's Ben Weatherstaff's robin. He's buildin' his nest. He'll stay here if us don't fight him." They settled down softly upon the grass and sat there without moving. . . .

Mistress Mary was not at all sure that she knew, as Dickon seemed to, how to try to look like grass and trees and bushes. But he had said the queer thing as if it were the simplest and most natural thing in the world, and she felt it must be quite easy to him, and indeed she watched him for a few minutes carefully, wondering if it was possible for him to quietly turn green and put out branches and leaves. But he only sat wonderfully still, and when he spoke dropped his voice to such a softness that it was curious that she could hear him, but she could.

"It's part o' th' springtime, this nest-buildin' is," he said. "I warrant it's been goin' on in th' same way every year since th' world was begun. They've got their way o' thinkin' and doin' things an' a body had better not meddle. You can lose a friend in springtime easier than any other season if you're too curious." . . .

He made one of his low whistling calls and the robin turned his head and looked at him inquiringly, still holding his twig. Dickon spoke to him as Ben Weatherstaff did, but Dickon's tone was one of friendly advice. . . .

"Tha' knows us won't trouble thee," he said to the robin. "Us is near bein' wild things ourselves. Us is nest-buildin' too, bless thee. Look out tha' doesn't tell on us."

And though the robin did not answer, because his beak was occupied, Mary knew that when he flew away with his twig to his own corner of the garden the darkness of his dew-bright eye meant that he would not tell their secret for the world.

 Questions

1. Why does Mary look different from when she first arrived from India?

    (A) She is happier.
    B   She is smarter.
    C   She is healthier.
    D   She has grown up.

 Tip

Think about the way Mary acts. Which conclusion is most likely?

2. Why doesn't Mary ask Colin the things she would like to know about him?

    (F) She doesn't want to be rude.
    G   She doesn't know if he'll be honest.
    H   She isn't sure if fresh air will be good for him.
    J   She isn't sure if Dickon will be upset with her.

 Tip

Carefully reread the beginning of the excerpt.

3. What can you tell about Dickon?

_____

_____

_____

_____

_____

_____

 **Tip**

What does Dickon do that is unusual?

Check your answers on the next page.

Passage 4: "Excerpt from *The Secret Garden*"

 Answers

1. A   Mary is much happier now. She is thrilled that it is spring and she values her friendship with Dickon. The narrator says that Mary looks nicer and remarks later in the excerpt that she notices things she would not have six months ago.

2. F   The beginning of the excerpt says that Mary feels she must find things out about Colin without asking him directly. This leads you to conclude that she doesn't want to offend him. Answer choice F is the best answer.

3. **Sample answer:** Dickon loves nature and has a unique way with animals that is likely unrealistic. He plays with and talks to a fox cub and a crow lands on his shoulder. He names these animals and considers them his friends.

 # Lesson 7: Critical Analysis and Fact and Opinion

New York State Learning Standard:

S3 Critical Analysis and Evaluation

Subskills:

Use critical analysis to evaluate information (S3)

Use critical analysis to evaluate ideas (S3)

Use critical analysis to recognize point of view (S3)

Distinguish between fact and opinion (S3)

What is critical analysis?

Critical analysis, or critical thinking, is a process that people use when they read something for the first time to help them comprehend what they have read. You should use critical-thinking skills every time you read something new, whether it's a test passage, a book, or a newspaper article. Anyone can sit down and read a paragraph, but to really understand it, you have to think critically about what it says. To think critically, you must try to relate new information to what you already know. Think about events in your own life and how your personal experiences relate to the new information. Look for key words or phrases in the reading and ask questions about topics you don't understand. Determine how the author feels about the subject of his or her writing.

Questions on the New York State test might also ask you to use critical analysis to distinguish between fact and opinion. A **fact** is a true statement that can be proven. The statement, "Rain falls from the sky" is a fact because it can be proven. An **opinion** is a judgment, or what someone thinks about something. Opinions often, but not always, begin with phrases such as "I think" or "I feel." The statement "I think rainy days make people sad" is an opinion because it cannot be proven. The statement "Rainy days are the worst" is also an opinion. Even though this statement doesn't say "I think" or "I feel," the person who wrote it is still making a judgment, or forming an opinion, about rainy days. When you think critically about a passage, try to determine which statements are fact, and which are opinions.

 Activity

Read the following adaptation of the familiar children's story "The Tortoise and the Hare." With a group of your classmates, make a list of facts from the story. Then make a list of opinions, and compare your results with the rest of your class.

The Tortoise and the Hare

Once upon a time, there lived a Hare who ran so fast that he looked like a blur, whizzing past his friends. The Hare often bragged about his speed.

"I'm the fastest animal in the whole forest," he claimed. "I can beat anyone in a race."

One day, the Tortoise heard the Hare talking about his amazing speed. Tortoises are known for moving very slowly. Even so, the Tortoise challenged the Hare to a race. The Hare laughed in the Tortoise's face. He knew he would win the race—he was the fastest animal in the forest.

The day of the race, all of the animals gathered to watch the Tortoise and the Hare. When the race started, the Hare was gone in a flash. He left poor Tortoise in the dust as he raced toward the finish line. But, the Tortoise didn't give up. He kept walking at his slow, steady pace. Eventually, the Hare turned around and could see the Tortoise was just a speck in the distance.

"I'm so far ahead, there's no way I can lose this race," the Hare said to himself. "I think I'll take a quick nap and rest up to celebrate my victory." The Hare sat beneath a tree and fell fast asleep.

The Tortoise kept trudging up the road. Finally, he saw the finish line in the distance. As he crossed the finish line, the animals cheered loudly. The Hare woke up to the sound of the cheering and realized what had happened. He dashed to the finish line, but it was too late. The Tortoise had won the race.

"You may be fast," said the Tortoise to the Hare, "but slow and steady wins the race."

Passage 1

Now read this passage. Use critical thinking skills and look for facts and opinions as you read. Then answer the questions that follow.

Cutting Class Size

"Falling through the cracks" sounds like a scary prospect, but overcrowding in American schools causes many students to slip through the cracks each day. Promising students get lost in the crowd and never receive the individual attention and stimulation they need to reach their full potential.

Fortunately, there is a solution to this problem. Reducing class size in America's schools is the best method by which we can eliminate these "cracks" in the educational system. This will be a challenging process, but many leading educators have developed a detailed plan to make it a reality.

The process should begin in the country's more troubled schools, where students' achievements have been consistently lower than average. These schools require special attention, and, by instituting small class size policies, they will receive it. With adequate funding, these troubled schools could hire more well-qualified teachers and provide additional classroom space for students. With more room and more teachers, the possibilities for these students are endless. Classes of fifteen to twenty students would be ideal, allowing more individual attention for each student.

Providing this reduced class size would greatly reduce many of the public's concerns about the United States' educational system. Students and parents alike have been worried by the sense of namelessness that exists in many modern schools. Under the current system, some students are just faces in a crowded classroom. However, the namelessness problem is not usually a teacher's fault. Many teachers work with over a hundred different students per day. It can be difficult to remember a hundred names, never mind personal details and small changes in individual students that might indicate more serious problems.

A reduction in class size could resolve these problems quickly. Teachers would have a much easier time getting to know their students' strengths and weaknesses, which can vastly improve a student's academic and personal experience. The teacher will be better able to help him or her, as well as communicate in more effective, meaningful ways.

For many students, the experience of attending overcrowded classes can be a miserable one. With thirty or more students confined in a small room, problems are inescapable. Yelling, fighting, or cheating, can make the classroom a stressful, depressing place to be, but teachers lack the time and resources they need to properly deal with these problems. With fewer students, there will almost certainly be reduced noise and distraction, making it easier for teachers to effectively guide the class.

Of course, there are people opposed to the idea of reducing class sizes in America's schools. These critics mostly point to the problem of funding these significant changes. Other critics say that creating smaller classes does not guarantee that students will improve their performance in school. However, it seems that a policy that allows students more access to instructors, and lets instructors become more familiar with students, promises to have a positive effect on our nation's schools.

Questions

1. List one fact and one opinion from the story.

_____

_____

2. In this passage, what does "falling through the cracks" mean?

_____

_____

_____

3. What might happen if teachers had fewer students in their classes?

_____

_____

_____

Check your answers on the next page.

Passage 1: "Cutting Class Size"

 **Answers**

1. One of your answers should be a true statement and the other one should be what someone thinks. Here is one example of each, but there are others!

   Fact: Many teachers work with over a hundred different students per day.

   Opinion: A reduction in class size could resolve these problems quickly.

2. Your answer should contain a phrase that explains what "falling through the cracks" means.

   Sample answer: Many students get overlooked because classes are large and there are not enough teachers.

3. Remember to think carefully about what you learned from the passage and about what you already know. The passage suggests that students "fall through the cracks" or get overlooked because classes are too large for teachers to handle.

   Sample answer: Students who were once overlooked will get the time and attention they need from teachers, and do better in school.

Passage 2

Now read this passage. Use critical thinking skills and look for facts and opinions as you read. Then answer the questions that follow.

The Dead Sea Scrolls

In 1947, a group of shepherds searching for a lost goat in the Judean Desert stumbled upon something amazing. They entered a deep cave that had been untouched for many years and discovered pottery jars containing parchment-paper scrolls—seven in all. While these shepherds could not decipher the information conveyed on the scrolls, they speculated that they were very old and of great value.

The shepherds sold the scrolls to someone, who sold them to someone else. The scrolls eventually caught the attention of American and European scholars, who identified them as ancient writings from people who once lived in Qumran, an ancient city near the Dead Sea, which is located in Israel and Jordan about fifteen miles east of Jerusalem.

About two years after the shepherds discovered the scrolls, archaeologists pinpointed the cave in which they were found and they dubbed this cave "Qumran Cave 1." Upon further exploration, archaeologists discovered additional scrolls in Cave 1 as well as fragments from scrolls dating back to 200 B.C.E to 68 C.E. Archaeologists unearthed other caves containing scrolls and fragments. These findings led to the excavation of Qumran in the 1950s. Approximately 900 scrolls, most of which were fragments, were discovered by archaeologists and others in eleven caves near Qumran.

What information is on the scrolls? They contain mostly religious myths and hymns. Archaeologists believe that the scrolls once comprised the library of a group of radical Jewish people, who hid in caves around the outbreak of the Jewish-Roman War (66 C.E.), but whose ancestors may have been living in and around these caves as early as 150 B.C.E The group, dubbed the "Dead Sea Sect," was intensely religious, conservative, and "hermit-like," rarely if ever socializing with others of their time.

 **Questions**

1. According to what you have read, archaeologists probably spent much time trying to

   A   determine why the scrolls were buried.
   B   piece together fragments of the scrolls.
   C   learn the hymns of the Dead Sea Sect.
   D   search for ancestors of the Dead Sea Sect.

 Tip

The Dead Sea Scrolls had been buried for centuries. Think about what the archaeologists probably had to do before they could begin translating the scrolls and learning what they said.

2. If you met a group of people from the Dead Sea Sect, they most likely would have

   F   sung you a hymn.
   G   showed you a cave.
   H   shied away from you.
   J   asked you to join them.

 Tip

Reread the last paragraph of the story. This paragraph provides clues as to how members of the Dead Sea Sect typically behaved. Choose an answer based on clues from the passage.

3. Why do you think the Dead Sea Scrolls were an important discovery?

_____

_____

_____

Check your answers on the next page.

Lesson 7   **CRITICAL ANALYSIS AND FACT AND OPINION**

Passage 2: "The Dead Sea Scrolls "

 # Answers

1. B   According to the passage, archaeologists found more than nine hundred scrolls, most of them in fragments. Before they could determine why the scrolls may have been buried or what they said, they had to piece the scrolls together to make the documents whole again. Answer B is correct.

2. H   The last paragraph of "The Dead Sea Scrolls" says that members of the Dead Sea Sect were 'hermit-like' and rarely socialized with others. Answer choice H is correct, because chances are that if you met a member of the Dead Sea Sect, they would have tried to avoid talking to you.

3.   **Sample answer:** The Dead Sea Scrolls were an important discovery because they were ancient and gave insight into a people who lived in the caves. They showed that these people were different from others of their time and that they had a library.

Passage 3

Now read this passage. Use critical thinking skills and look for facts and opinions as you read. Then answer the questions that follow.

The "Reality" of Reality Television

The American people have suffered long enough: it's time to put an end to reality television. In recent years, reality television shows have become a staple of many networks' programming schedules and it's easy to see why. Reality television offers a glimpse into the lives of people just like you and me. Rather than watching a scripted television show where a famous actor or actress portrays a normal, ordinary person, we can watch normal, ordinary people receive the star treatment, compete in outrageous contests, and win exorbitant amounts of money. Who wouldn't want to live in a "reality" where you can increase your bank account by a few thousand dollars simply by swimming with a few snakes or parachuting out of a plane?

Reality television does have some advantages over traditional scripted television shows. There seems to be an endless supply of topics from which to choose, and an endless number of people willing to step up and take on the newest challenge. There's always some new show waiting in the wings, ready to humiliate a new cast of characters and spark the interest of a new group of viewers. From the corporate world to operating tables to boxing rings, it seems that reality television cameras are everywhere, witnessing everything. As long as the cameras catch a few laughs, a few cries, and a few fights, producers can take months of footage and piece together several hours of fast-paced, exciting television. Reality shows take less time, effort, and money to create than scripted television shows. There's usually one big pay-off at the end of the show where the winner gets an amazing prize, instead of five or six actors and actresses who are paid high salaries per episode. Despite these few positive aspects, most reality television shows are littered with problems.

Perhaps the main problem with reality television is best demonstrated through a comparison of actual reality and television reality. In the early days of film, filmmakers created documentaries about real people and events in history. For example, a filmmaker might show how Inuit people living in Alaska hunt for caribou. Another filmmaker might capture the ancient rituals of an African tribe or show the effects of poverty in a Third World country. When these documentaries were shown on television, viewers could see how ordinary people living in the real world are affected by real circumstances. These documentaries served as educational tools by showing the actual reality that some people must face. The difference between this reality and today's reality television shows

is that today's shows have lost the concept of "reality." Reality shows that set out to represent real life situations that could affect anyone at any time have morphed into outrageous contests that focus on the extremes people will go to get what they want. Can it be considered "reality" to drop a bunch of strangers on an island with no food or water and force them to compete for a million dollars? Is it reality to participate in all kinds of crazy tests in order to be crowned the head of a successful corporation? Television reality shows are less about real life and more about the best way to surprise a member of the cast and shock viewers at home.

Today's reality shows no longer offer us a real glimpse into the lives of people and cultures from around the world. We don't get to see how people really live, work, and interact with others. We don't get to hear their innermost thoughts and feelings, or see their ways of life. Instead, most of today's reality television shows offer viewers a cast of characters who live in a tent, on an island, or in some magnificent mansion. These people participate in funny, foolish, or outlandish acts to win money, cars, jobs, modeling contracts, recording contracts, and even future spouses. They will do whatever it takes to have their fifteen minutes of fame. These shows pit friend against friend, husband against wife, and family against family, all in the name of entertainment. But what happens when these shows are over and these people try to return to their normal lives? Is it possible for them to go back to their old lives when their words and actions are immortalized on the television screen for the whole world to see?

It is a shame that this form of television, which could be used to educate the world about so many important issues, is more often used as an expanded dating game or the road to superstardom. Instead of teaching us about the reality of what it's like to grow up in a minority, reality shows teach us how to put a puzzle together with our toes while wearing a blindfold. Reality shows could focus on important issues that people deal with in real life: finding a job after high school or college; volunteering for a community organization; or learning how to perform a new skill. Instead, most "reality shows" give us a group of people taking time out from their normal, everyday lives to take part in some fantastic scheme created by a television producer. And the last time I checked, that wasn't reality.

 Questions

1. The author would probably agree with which statement?

   A   Reality shows are educational and entertaining.
   B   Most reality shows depict real people living ordinary lives.
   C   People should be forced to tell the truth on reality shows.
   D   Reality shows are more about playing games than living life.

 Tip

Think about the author's purpose in writing this passage. Think about the main idea of the passage and the details the author uses to support the main idea. Use these clues to help you determine the author's point of view.

CRITICAL ANALYSIS AND FACT AND OPINION   Lesson 7

2. Which of the following statements from the passage is an opinion?

    F   Reality television offers a glimpse into the lives of people just like you and me.

    G   Despite these few positive aspects, most reality television shows are littered with problems.

    H   In the early days of film, filmmakers created documentaries about real people and events in history.

    J   These documentaries served as educational tools by showing the actual reality that some people must face.

 Tip

Remember that a fact is a true statement that can be proven and an opinion is what a person thinks about something. Which answer choice expresses what someone thinks about reality television?

3. How might the words and actions of a reality show star affect their lives when the show is over?

_____

_____

_____

_____

 Tip

Think about home movies you might have that show you saying or doing something funny or silly. Now think about reality shows. What people say and do on these shows will be shown to people across the nation.

4. Why is the title of this passage appropriate?

    A   It hints that reality shows might not be realistic.

    B   It makes readers question the validity of television.

    C   It shocks the reader by making an outrageous statement.

    D   It gives insight into how the author feels about reality shows.

 Tip

Reread the title of the passage. Then think about the meaning of the passage. Why is the title appropriate?

Check your answers on the next page.

Lesson 7 **CRITICAL ANALYSIS AND FACT AND OPINION**

Passage 3: "The 'Reality' of Reality Television"

 Answers

1. D   Answer choice D is correct. The author mentions several times in the passage that reality shows often make contestants compete in foolish games to win prizes. The author also mentions that most reality shows lack educational value. However, the author would not want to ban a show that truly depicts real-life problems and situations.

2. G   Answer choice G is correct because it is the only choice that expresses an opinion. All of the other answer choices are factual statements that do not contain judgments by the author.

3.   **Sample answer:** When a reality show is over, contestants must return to their normal lives. During the show, they sometimes say things or do things that offend or hurt people, and those words or actions are preserved forever.

4. A   The title of this passage is appropriate because it uses the definition of reality sarcastically. In doing this, it hints that the reality shows may not be realistic. Answer choice A is the best answer.

Passage 4

Now read this passage. Use critical thinking skills and look for facts and opinions as you read. Then answer the questions that follow.

The Loose Law of the Library
Schools That Don't Protect Their Students

A topic that has recently stirred debate is the issue of censorship in school libraries. Recently, a sixth-grade student at Gerald Hoover Middle School in California was scanning the school library's shelves for reference materials for a research paper when she came across a book containing graphic images inappropriate for children. The student was disturbed by these images and presented the book to the school librarian, who simply re-shelved the book and dismissed the student's concerns. Many parents feel that the school's response to this student's concerns is insufficient and irresponsible.

While the issue of censorship is a heated one in which people express many different opinions, responsible adults should monitor the materials that children have access to while in school. This does not mean that we need library-wide censorship. Public libraries have a duty to follow the Library Bill of Rights and provide readers with a wide range of materials. Though students may access materials considered inappropriate for children at the public library, it is not the library's responsibility to monitor what children are reading—it is the parents' responsibility. Parents can accompany their children into the public library and help their children choose reading materials that they consider to be appropriate for their children. Parents cannot, however, do this is school libraries, and this is where the school, as a responsible educational institution, must step in.

Parents send their children off to school every day with the knowledge that they will be educated, protected, and cared for to the best of the school's ability. Schools do not allow harmful materials such as weapons or illegal substances into schools, and they should not allow harmful reading materials either. When parents brought their personal concerns to the Gerald Hoover Middle School librarian, she told them that preventing students from accessing certain reading materials would be an abuse of their rights. However, if it is in fact a right that students be permitted to view whatever materials have been made available to them, then this is a right that must be abused in order to protect the children. Many American laws are designed to protect those not old enough to make intelligent informed decisions, those who have not lived long enough or gained enough world experience to be responsible for themselves. When our children age and mature, they are given more freedom to make their own choices based on what they have learned while under our protective wings. Reading materials loaded with mature subject matter should be reserved for mature people, not sixth and seventh graders.

Children see things much differently than adults do. When a youngster views materials that are intended for adults, he or she is looking at the pictures and interpreting the text as a child, through a child's limited worldview. He or she does not always have the intellectual or emotional capacity to understand what is being read. An adult reading the same text is much more equipped to interpret and understand such mature subject matter. The same principle applies to different forms of information and entertainment, such as television shows, movies, and video games, whose content is all rated according to its appropriateness for different age groups. Many shows and movies containing graphic violence or nudity are deemed inappropriate for children, who cannot always understand what they are seeing, or who may mimic what they see, as is the nature of growing youngsters. Most can probably agree that not every television program, movie, or video game is suitable for young children, so why are books different? Do librarians and educators truly believe that no book could harm a child, simply because it is a book? If certain images and subject matters are considered inappropriate in their video form, then why are they acceptable for children when put into print form? If children are not emotionally or intellectually mature enough to handle what they encounter, the results can be harmful and severe.

As previously stated, monitoring reading materials in a public library is a parent's job. When children are not in school, their parents are responsible for looking after them and caring for them, but because parents cannot accompany their children to school, school educators and administrators often step into many of the roles and responsibilities undertaken by parents. Students are fed, provided with intellectual and physical activities, and disciplined when necessary, so why, then, should the school be exempt from the responsibility of monitoring the reading materials to which our children are exposed? Should all concerned parents pull their students out of schools and educate them at home so that they are protected in a way that the schools cannot—or will not—do? This is not the best answer, but it shows that when schools will not take responsibility for protecting their students, some type of parental action is necessary.

The inappropriate materials on the shelves of school libraries should be formally reviewed, beginning with the one book that we know has had a detrimental effect on at least one of the school's students—the one that still sits on the shelves of Gerald Hoover Middle School, available to all students. The school library has a materials selection policy, and the board of education makes the final decisions about library materials. While their intentions are likely good ones, they have obviously let a few inappropriate materials slip through the cracks, and so parents cannot be sure that their children are not reading books too mature for their years. While academic and intellectual freedoms are important, they are only beneficial to children when exercised responsibly, and those running the school in question have proved themselves irresponsible in this respect. Perhaps school libraries need additional safeguards on mature materials, such as a separate section of the library for mature materials, which students would need to present student identification verifying their ages in order to enter. Or perhaps schools need to put control back in the hands of the parents by requiring parents to sign a form stating whether or not their child is permitted to access mature materials in the school library. Whatever the answer, it is clear that change is necessary for the safety of schoolchildren.

CRITICAL ANALYSIS AND FACT AND OPINION　Lesson 7

 Questions

1. According to what you have read, allowing a child to view inappropriate materials in a school library can be best compared to

   A removing ratings on movies in theaters
   B leaving a child unsupervised in a busy place
   C allowing too many children in one classroom
   D allowing children to dine in a restaurant without parents

 Tip

Choose the answer choice that is most similar to allowing children to see inappropriate materials in a school library. Reread the author's suggestions for reducing the risk that this will happen.

2. Why does the author include the story of the sixth-grade student at Gerald Hoover Middle School?

   F to show that some schools are unconcerned about this issue
   G to prove that children often see inappropriate reading materials
   H to suggest that parents are eager to get involved in the situation
   J to imply that children do not want to have access to such materials

 Tip

Reread the introduction of this passage. Think about the point the author is trying to make.

3. Why might a parent be upset to learn that the school library has inappropriate material on its shelves?

_____

_____

_____

 Tip

Use details from the passage to support your answer.

Check your answers on the next page.

Passage 4: "The Loose Law of the Library"

 Answers

1. A   Removing the ratings on movie theaters is closely related to not screening books in a school library. The other answer choices have nothing to do with reviewing something to determine if it is suitable for children.

2. F   The author includes this anecdote to show that the student was upset and the librarian simply re-shelved the book. Answer choice J also seems like a good answer choice, but this story does not indicate that all students would be upset by such materials. However, it does show that some schools are unconcerned about the issue.

3.   **Sample answer:** Parents might be upset to learn that the library contained material unsuitable for children, because when they send their children to school, they expect them to return home safe and sound. They expect that their children are spending the day in a safe environment where they will stay out of trouble. At home, parents can regulate what their children see and are exposed to, but at school they cannot. Parents send their children to school thinking that they will be protected by school officials, faculty, and staff, but instead of being in a safe environment, their children are being exposed to harmful images or words.

Lesson 8: Writing

New York State Learning Standard:

S4 Read, write, listen and speak for social interaction

The New York State test asks you to answer an extended-response question. For these questions, you will compose an essay in response to a writing prompt. The purpose of this question is to test your writing skills.

Writing is an important aspect of daily life. People write to communicate their thoughts and ideas to others. They may write to provide information on an interesting topic, to analyze or evaluate an issue, to give opinions about something, or simply to stay in touch with old friends.

When you begin to write anything, from an essay to a story to a friendly letter, you should use the process of prewriting, drafting, revising, and proofreading. During the **prewriting** stage, you should brainstorm different ideas and determine what you would like to write about. Think about the audience you will be writing for and the purpose of your writing. Are you trying to entertain readers with a story, give your opinion, or interpret something in your own words? Once you have determined your central idea, purpose, and audience, jot down some supporting material and organize or outline your ideas into a logical sequence. Then begin the drafting stage.

In the **drafting** stage, you will begin writing a rough draft of your work. An important thing to remember when writing your draft is to get your ideas down on paper. This stage of your writing does not have to be perfect. It is acceptable for the rough draft to have mistakes. These mistakes can be changed or fixed during the revising stage of writing.

When your rough draft is finished, it's time to begin **revising** and **proofreading** your work. Read your rough draft carefully. Look for mistakes in grammar, spelling, punctuation, and capitalization, and look for sentence fragments. Make sure that you have stated your main idea or that you have provided enough supporting details for readers to determine the central theme. Reword sentences or move entire paragraphs to make your writing flow in a clear, logical order. Add more details to make your writing vibrant and exciting. Once you are happy with your revised draft, proofread your work to make sure it is completely error-free. When you have finished proofreading, rewrite the final copy of your work in your best handwriting.

Writer's checklist

_____ Focus on the main idea of your writing and think about your audience.

_____ Support your main idea with interesting facts and details.

_____ Organize your ideas in a logical sequence that best communicates what you are trying to say.

_____ Vary the length and structure of your sentences.

_____ Know the meanings of the words you choose, and use them correctly.

_____ Check the basics. Make sure your capitalization, punctuation, and spelling are correct.

_____ Use your best handwriting for the final copy of your writing.

WRITING A GOOD ESSAY

In order to achieve the highest score for your essay, use the process of prewriting, drafting, revising, and proofreading. Also, pay attention to the content and organization of your essay, as well as usage, sentence construction, and mechanics.

Content/Organization: When you write, you should frame the body of your composition with strong opening and closing ideas. Make sure that you have addressed the reasons that your issue is important, and include a conclusion as to why you feel the way you do about the issue.

In between the opening and closing of your composition are your main ideas. Make sure that your ideas are clear, and that you have included a variety of main ideas and have not simply stressed the same point multiple times. Your ideas should follow a logical progression, meaning that transition from one main idea to another should not be choppy, but instead should flow easily from one idea to the next. Your ideas should also be supported by details, facts, opinions, comparisons, and contrasts. Be sure that your transitions from opening to main ideas to closing are fluid instead of choppy.

Sentence Construction: Make sure that you follow traditional grammar rules when composing sentences. You should check to make sure that you have placed periods and commas in logical places. You should also make sure that all of your sentences are not structured the same way. Variety will make your composition better.

Usage: When you revise and proofread, make sure that you use correct verb tense and agreement. For example, if you are using past-tense verbs to describe something that happened in the past, then make sure that all verbs to describe this past event are set in the past tense. Also, look at your pronouns (*I, you, he, she, it, we, they*) to make sure that you have used them correctly. Examine your composition to make sure you have used words that will engage your audience. If you don't like the look or sound of a certain word in your composition, try to replace it with a better one.

Mechanics: Mechanics are the spelling, capitalization, and punctuation in your composition. If you are not sure of the spelling or capitalization of a word, look it up in the dictionary. Even though no one will see your oral composition, if the mechanics are correct, it will be easier for you to deliver your speech than it would be if your speech text contains mechanical errors.

SAMPLE PROMPT

The principal of your school has recently announced that all students will be required to wear a uniform next year. Girls will wear white shirts and navy blue skirts, and boys will wear white shirts and navy blue pants. Some students in your school think uniforms are a good idea because they create a sense of equality between all students. Others think that wearing a uniform will hinder their creativity and individuality.

Write an essay arguing either for or against the new uniform policy. Be sure to support your statements with details, facts, and opinions.

SAMPLE ANSWER

Last week, officials at Middletown Junior High School created a new policy requiring all students to wear a uniform to school to next year. I can understand how school officials might think that uniforms create a sense of equality among students, but I also believe that people often dress to show off a part of their personality. Taking away a student's right to choose his or her own clothes destroys their sense of individuality. Who wants to live in a world where everyone looks and dresses the same way?

The school already imposes a dress code for students, and students who break the dress code are given detention. I believe that as long as students are following the dress code, they should be allowed to wear whatever they want. People often choose clothes based on the mood they are in when the wake up. If a person is sad, he or she might choose clothes that make them feel and look good as a way of brightening his or her day. If a person is feeling sick or tired, he or she might choose clothes that make him or her feel comfortable and cozy. If students are forced to wear uniforms, they will not have this option.

In addition, some students are known for their unique sense of style, and forcing them to wear a uniform will take away part of their personality. For example, one of my classmates sews her own clothes. These clothes are beautiful, well-made, and admired by all. When people mention her name, they often mention her fashion sense. By forcing her to wear a uniform, she will become just another face in the sea of white and navy blue. Other students are known for their silly t-shirts, their football jerseys, or their letterman's jackets. You can often tell by looking at a person's clothes whether that person's personality is funny, serious, athletic, or outgoing. In uniforms, each person in this school will look exactly like every other person in this school. The creativity and individuality that we now find fun, exciting, and stimulating will be gone.

Part 1: Reading

Directions

The following article describes an ancient Mesopotamian burial ground. Read "The Royal Cemetery at Ur." Then answer questions 1 through 5 on the answer sheet on page 187.

The Royal Cemetery at Ur

In the 1920s, a team of archaeologists led by Sir Leonard Woolley made an amazing discovery. They excavated an ancient cemetery in what was once Mesopotamia, an area between the Tigris and Euphrates Rivers, most of which is now modern-day Iraq, Kuwait, and Saudi Arabia. The cemetery was located in the ancient Sumerian city-state Ur, which existed over 3,000 years ago. The Sumerians used the cemetery for over five hundred years and it contained about 1,800 bodies and many ancient artifacts. Archaeologists have learned a great deal about the Sumerians and life in ancient times from studying the contents of burial tombs at Ur.

Most people buried in the Royal Cemetery at Ur were common citizens whose funeral rites consisted of merely wrapping their bodies in a reed mat before burial. About sixteen bodies were buried in "royal tombs," large elaborate underground structures with several rooms called chambers. Royal families—kings, queens, and their families—were buried in these tombs. The Sumerians closely intertwined politics and religion and they considered these individuals to be of great importance. Each Sumerian city-state was ruled by a king, who was also a priest. The Sumerians believed that everything around them was controlled by a god. They believed that the sun, moon, and stars were gods. They also believed that their kings were gods and that they were put on the earth to serve them. They built magnificent burial chambers for their kings and queens because they thought this would please them.

The Sumerians believed that kings and queens could take things with them on their journey to the afterlife. They filled royal tombs with everything they thought people would need on this journey, including

Go On

clothes, jewelry, riches, weapons—and even people. It was not uncommon for Sumerian citizens to sacrifice themselves because they believed this would allow them to accompany their king in the afterlife, where they could continue to serve him.

Perhaps the most amazing discovery in the Cemetery at Ur was Queen Puabi's tomb. The queen's tomb was especially valuable because it was discovered intact, meaning it had not been disturbed since the Sumerians closed it thousands of years ago. While Queen Puabi's tomb was built on top of another burial chamber, probably the king's, not much is known about the king, because his tomb was *looted*, or robbed, many years ago, probably when the queen was buried.

Queen Puabi's tomb was extraordinary and demonstrated the Sumerians' advanced skills in architectural design. Her body was laid to rest on a table in the middle of an arched chamber in the center of what archaeologists refer to as a death pit. The pit and her burial chamber were filled with exquisite ancient artifacts. Queen Puabi was adorned with an incredible headdress made of gold leaves, ribbons, and strands of beads made from rare stones. She wore a cylinder seal around her neck bearing her name. Her name was carved into the cylinder using cuneiform, the world's first written language, which was invented by the Sumerians. The queen's body was covered in a beaded cape made from precious metals and stone. The cape stretched from her shoulders to her waist. Beautiful rings were carefully placed on each of her fingers.

Members of the queen's "burial party" were discovered in the death pit. Members of this burial party apparently accompanied the queen into her tomb. Each member of the party dressed formally for the special occasion and enjoyed an enormous feast prior to joining Queen Puabi. The burial party included more than a dozen attendants or servants, five armed men, a wooden sled, and a pair of oxen. Four grooms were buried with the oxen, possibly to care for the oxen in the afterlife.

What happened to the members of the burial party to cause their demise? No one is sure, since they died thousands of years ago. However, Sir Woolley and his teams discovered a gold cup near each of their bodies. They suspect that the attendants probably drank poison so they could go to sleep forever alongside their queen, who may or may not have been already dead.

Go On

1 What covered Queen Puabi's body?

A a cylinder seal

B a beaded cape

C wooden planks

D gold leaves and ribbons

2 What is the primary topic of the second paragraph of the article?

F Queen Puabi's tomb

G common Sumerian citizens

H the royal tombs in the cemetery

J the importance of Sumerian kings

3 Why did the Sumerians build elaborate burial tombs for the kings?

A They believed their kings were gods.

B They hoped to serve their kings in the afterlife.

C They thought their kings would return one day.

D They wanted to protect their kings from thieves.

4 What was the author's purpose in writing this article?

F to explain what it was like to be a Sumerian

G to teach readers about Queen Puabi's tomb

H to inform readers about an ancient discovery

J to convince readers of the Sumerians' greatness

5 You can conclude from this passage that the queen's tomb might have been robbed if—

A someone had been buried on top of her chamber.

B her attendants were not buried with her.

C her tomb was smaller than the king's tomb.

D if it had not been discovered by Sir Woolley.

Go On

***D**irections*

Read the following poem. Then answer questions 6 through 10 on the answer sheet on page 187.

Chicago Poet

by Carl Sandburg
(*from Cornhuskers, Henry Holt, 1918*)

I saluted a nobody.
I saw him in a looking-glass.
He smiled—so did I.
He crumpled the skin on his forehead, frowning—so did I.
Everything I did he did.
I said, "Hello, I know you."
And I was a liar to say so.

Ah, this looking-glass man!
Liar, fool, dreamer, play-actor,
Soldier, dusty drinker of dust—
Ah! he will go with me
Down the dark stairway
When nobody else is looking,
When everybody else is gone.

He locks his elbow in mine,
I lose all—but not him.

Go On

6 The wording of the poem shows that the poet is

    F sitting alone in the dark.

    G looking at his reflection in a mirror.

    H writing about several different people.

    J having a conversation with another man.

7 Which of the following best describes the man in the looking-glass?

    A a brave warrior

    B a foolish idealist

    C a faithful companion

    D an enthusiastic teacher

8 When will the man in the looking-glass go with the poet?

    F at nighttime

    G when he is tired

    H when he is alone

    J during the next day

9 What is the overall tone of the poem?

    A weary

    B angry

    C relieved

    D speculative

10 In the poem, the author loses

    F the looking-glass

    G his sense of humor

    H his way in the dark

    J everything but himself

Go On

*D*irections

Read the following article about the history of drive-in movie theaters. Then answer questions 11 through 15 on the answer sheet on page 187.

The History of Drive-in Theaters

When people go to the movies they are often greeted by long lines at the ticket counter, expensive refreshments, and a sticky floor beneath their feet. One way to skip those aggravations and still enjoy the latest blockbuster hit is to go to a drive-in theater. Back in the late 1940s and 1950s, open-air cinemas, or "ozoners," peaked in popularity. Drive-in theaters were an inexpensive way for families to enjoy a movie in the comfort of their own vehicles. They could load the car with snacks, drinks, and blankets, and settle in for a feature film on a warm summer night. They could talk, joke, and laugh in the privacy of their own car without the fear of being shushed by someone sitting a few rows back.

The First Drive-in Theater

The first drive-in theater was invented by Richard Hollingshead, a young sales manager from Camden, New Jersey, who wanted to create a way for people to enjoy movies from their cars. He experimented with this idea by mounting a movie projector on the hood of his car and aiming it at a white sheet attached to trees in his yard. Placing a radio behind the sheet for sound, he had the basic ideas for his open-air cinema in place, but Hollingshead strove to make it better. He worried that bad weather might affect the picture, so he used hoses and lawn sprinklers to simulate a rainstorm. The next problem he faced was parking. When one car parked right behind another, the view of the screen was partially blocked. By spacing the cars apart and parking the rear cars on blocks and ramps, Hollingshead discovered a way for all moviegoers to view the screen without a problem. With his idea perfected, Hollingshead obtained a patent for an open-air cinema on May 16, 1933, and less than one month later, he opened the first drive-in theater in Camden. Three large speakers broadcast sound while the screen displayed the picture. The cost for a drive-in movie was twenty-five cents for the car and twenty-five cents for each person.

An Uphill Climb for Drive-in Theaters

It didn't take long before other drive-in theaters were built. By 1942, there were about a hundred drive-in theaters across the United States, but World War II slowed this growth. Gasoline, rubber, and metal were all rationed for the war effort, and it wasn't until the war ended that the number of open-air cinemas increased. By 1948, the number of drive-in theaters had risen to 820.

A number of factors contributed to the rising popularity of drive-in theaters, one being the improved technology for sound. Gone were the days of bullhorn speakers mounted to the screen. Instead, drive-in theaters used in-car speakers that allowed moviegoers to adjust the volume to their liking. The baby boom also contributed to the popularity of open-air cinemas. In the years following World War II, mainly the 1940s and 1950s, there was a sharp increase in the number of babies born in the United States. As the number of families with children

Go On

grew, outdoor cinemas became more family friendly. Theater owners built playgrounds where toddlers and young children could play before the movie started. Some cinemas became small amusement parks offering pony rides, train rides, miniature golf, talent shows, and of course, refreshments. By the end of the 1940s, open-air cinemas had surpassed indoor cinemas in popularity. They reached their peak in 1958, with more than four thousand outdoor screens showing movies across the country.

Cruising to the Concession Stand

Refreshment stands have long been a staple of the drive-in movie industry. Offering a variety of foods from hot dogs, hamburgers, and French fries, to assorted candy and beverages, refreshment stands were often responsible for a large amount of drive-in theaters' profits. In the early days, some outdoor cinemas had "carhops," waiters and waitresses who brought food right to your car window. Other cinemas went with a more traditional cafeteria-style refreshment stand, while some larger theaters offered restaurants with full meals. To increase refreshment sales even more, theaters began showing intermission trailers, or "clocks," between films. These trailers were short, ten- to twenty-minute, animated films featuring dancing snacks and drinks that enticed moviegoers to head to the concession stand. They often had a clock somewhere on the screen counting down the time to the start of the next film.

Drive-in Theaters Hit a Roadblock

Just as quickly as they rose to popularity, drive-in theaters began a downward slide. Through the 1960s their numbers remained fairly constant, but the audience changed. Fewer families attended drive-in movies, so cinemas began targeting a teen audience with movies unsuitable for young children. In the 1970s, property values began to increase and many theaters closed to make room for shopping centers. Large indoor theaters offered the newest movies on multiple screens, and outdoor cinemas suffered.

In addition, cable television and videocassette recorders (VCRs) were introduced. These inventions brought Hollywood movies into people's homes. They no longer had to drive to a theater, buy tickets and snacks, and find a place to park. They simply turned on the television or popped in a videotape. By 1983, there were less than three thousand drive-in theaters in the country.

Reversing the Trend

Throughout the 1990s, many open-air cinemas continued to close. Less than six hundred drive-in theaters and 815 screens remained in operation in the United States by 1997. Good news is on the horizon, however. In recent years, some drive-in theaters have reopened, new open-air cinemas have been built, and families are beginning to attend the outdoor pictures once again. These families will treasure the experience as much as those of the past.

Go On

11 What was the most profitable aspect of drive-in theaters for those who owned them?

A   fees charged per person

B   fees charged per car load

C   money spent at playgrounds

D   money spent on food and drinks

12 Which statement is an opinion from the passage?

F   By 1983, there were less than three thousand drive-in theaters in the country.

G   These families will treasure the experience as much as those of the past.

H   These trailers were short, ten- to twenty-minute, animated films featuring dancing snacks and drinks that enticed moviegoers to head to the concession stand.

J   To increase refreshment sales even more, theaters began showing intermission trailers, or "clocks," between films.

13 Many people in the 1980s did <u>not</u> visit drive-in theaters because

A   they had a hard time seeing the screen

B   they couldn't hear the bullhorn speakers

C   they didn't want to see children's movies

D   they had video cassette recorders in their homes

14 Which quotation best supports the author's argument that an effort was made in the 1940s and 1950s to make drive-in theaters more family friendly?

F   "Refreshment stands have long been a staple of the drive-in movie industry."

G   "Drive-in theaters used in-car speakers that allowed moviegoers to adjust the volume to their liking."

H   "Theater owners built playgrounds where toddlers and young children could play before the movie started."

J   "In the early days, some outdoor cinemas had 'carhops,' waiters or waitresses who brought food right to your car window."

15 According to what you have read, the fading popularity of drive-in theaters in the 1970s and 1980s can best be compared to the popularity of

A   movies

B   fast food

C   the Internet

D   radio dramas

Go On

*D*irections

Look at the flyer for a special community service that can keep pets safe. Then answer questions 16 through 18 on the answer sheet on page 187.

Westchester County SPCA
Microchip Clinic

Where: Westchester County SPCA
305 Sullivan Avenue
White Plains, NY

When: Saturday, June 7
9:00 a.m. to 5:00 p.m.

Cost: Free!

A Microchip May Bring a Lost Pet Home
Many dogs and cats are lost in Westchester County each year, and, sadly, some of these beloved pets are never reunited with their owners. To keep this from happening, the Westchester County SPCA is holding a free microchip clinic for cats and dogs.

A microchip is a great tool to reveal a pet's identity. While the Westchester County SPCA strongly recommends that all animals wear a collar with an identification tag, a microchip provides a safety net in case an animal becomes separated from its collar and identification tag. Once a microchip is implanted under a pet's skin—and it doesn't hurt a bit!—it is good for the life of your pet.

How Microchipping Works
When a lost pet is picked up by an animal control officer or a concerned citizen and is brought to the shelter, the animal is scanned by shelter professionals using a hand-held scanner. If a microchip has been implanted in the animal, the skin reflects the signal given by the scanner and provides a unique alpha-numeric code. This code is entered into a computer and the animal's owner is revealed.

Need More Information?
Telephone or visit the Westchester County SPCA. Our professional staff will be happy to answer your questions. (555) 274-9807.

Go On

16 The service provided by this flyer is mainly intended to

F inform people of an upcoming event

G explain the process of microchipping

H describe the benefits of microchipping

J persuade people to keep their pets safe

17 How does this flyer organize its information?

A giving step-by-step instructions

B providing a question-and-answer format

C sorting topics under appropriate headlines

D listing the benefits and hazards of microchipping

18 This flyer gives all of the following information EXCEPT

F the name of a contact person

G the hours of the microchip clinic

H a brief description of microchipping

J assurance that a pet won't be injured

Directions

Many legends exist about the Babylonian hero King Gilgamesh. Read this adaptation of one of his adventures. Then answer questions 19 through 25 on the answer sheet on page 187.

THE MYTH OF KING GILGAMESH

Thousands of years ago, the people of ancient Babylonia had great respect for their king, Gilgamesh. He was the son of powerful gods and had superhuman strength. Gilgamesh had keen intelligence and great foresight. He oversaw the construction of Uruk, a beautiful city.

However, Gilgamesh had many flaws. He was arrogant and brash, and frequently neglected the needs of his people in favor of his own desires. He was also oppressive and demanded complete control of everyone in his kingdom. When he began to interfere in people's weddings, the people of Babylonia decided that something had to be done. They flocked to their temple and prayed to their chief god, Anu, pleading with him to confront Gilgamesh and end his exploitation. Their prayers were answered with silence, however, and they left the temple disappointed.

The next day, a hunter named Shuja headed into the forests outside of the city in search of game. As soon as he stepped into the thick, shadowy woods, he heard the roar of an animal he did not recognize. It resembled a horrifying combination of the growls, hoots, whistles, and barks of a dozen different species. He heard it again, and it was closer this time. Before he could flee, he found himself face-to-face with a hulking wild man surrounded by a team of vicious animals.

An hour later, an exhausted Shuja returned to the city. He looked so ragged and terrified that a crowd gathered around him, inquiring what troubles had befallen him. "I encountered a wild man in the forest training animals for warfare," Shuja explained. "His name was Enkidu, and he said Anu had dispatched him to dethrone King Gilgamesh."

A worried murmur passed through the crowd. *What would happen if such a menacing creature attacked Uruk?* they wondered. The prospect was even less pleasant than living under Gilgamesh's continued oppression. They realized they needed to stop Enkidu, but how could they negotiate with an animal-like man? Some thought they should fight. Others thought they should flee. Still others thought they should surrender to the creature and try to reason with it. Nobody could agree on a course of action.

Go On

"Stop this quarrelling. I'll get us out of this predicament," announced Shamhat, one of the most beautiful women in Uruk. The next morning she left the city's protective walls and proceeded into the forest in search of Enkidu. She found him at a watering hole where he and his supporters had stopped to rest. Shamhat approached him confidently, and he could sense that she was not motivated by apprehension or hostility. This caught Enkidu off guard.

Shamhat addressed Enkidu with kindness and compassion, and he responded in a similarly civil manner. They spent the day together and, the next morning, she led him into Uruk as a friend, not an enemy. The people gathered around them and celebrated the cessation of this threat. Enkidu, though disoriented by the new environment, came to love the beauty, companionship, and sophistication he encountered inside the city walls. Taking up residence with some shepherds, Enkidu learned how to behave like a civilized human being.

Meanwhile, Gilgamesh had been having visions of powerful, mysterious newcomers trespassing upon his land. It was therefore no surprise to him to learn of Enkidu's presence in Uruk. Gilgamesh consulted with his mother, who advised him to embrace this newcomer as a friend, because together they were destined for great accomplishments.

What does she know? Gilgamesh thought bitterly. *I would not degrade myself by accepting some wild man as a companion.*

And so Gilgamesh continued his oppression of the people. During a marriage celebration, Gilgamesh interfered again. He was jealous of the groom and intended to kidnap the bride. He believed he was justified in doing so because he was the ruler of Uruk, and he was comfortable with the knowledge that nobody would challenge him. But he had forgotten about the newcomer, Enkidu, who suddenly appeared in the king's doorway and refused to allow him to break up the wedding.

"How dare you exploit your people for your own gain!" demanded Enkidu.

"How dare you question my decisions!" roared Gilgamesh, lunging forward to attack his challenger.

The two combatants struggled for hours, their powers equally balanced. Finally, Gilgamesh was able to secure an advantage by raising a sword high over Enkidu. Instead of bringing the sword slashing down, however, he paused and then slowly lowered the weapon.

"You are a worthy opponent," he admitted, "and I was wrong to belittle you. I see the wisdom in your challenge, and I will not spoil the wedding." Gilgamesh helped Enkidu to his feet, and they shook hands. "I think my mother was right. If you and I work together, we can accomplish great things for the people of Uruk."

Go On

19 Gilgamesh began to respect Enkidu after

A exploring Enkidu's past

B deciding to ignore his mother

C asking the people for their advice

D learning that Enkidu was a mighty warrior

20 Why were the people of Babylon upset with King Gilgamesh?

F He forbade them to pray to Anu.

G He listened to his mother's advice.

H He made friends with a wild man.

J He interfered in wedding ceremonies.

21 Why does the author record Gilgamesh's thoughts after he speaks with his mother?

A to show that Gilgamesh is keeping secrets

B to explain Gilgamesh's immediate reaction

C to suggest that Gilgamesh is afraid to speak

D to contrast Gilgamesh's attitude with his mother's

22 Read this sentence from the story:

The people gathered around them and celebrated the cessation of this threat.

In this sentence, what does *cessation* mean?

F end

G increase

H meaning

J alteration

23 Early in the story, Gilgamesh would probably agree with which statement?

A Might makes right.

B Mother knows best.

C Power to the people.

D All humans are created equal.

24 Why didn't Gilgamesh want to make friends with Enkidu?

F He was afraid of Enkidu.

G His mother warned against it.

H He knew Enkidu wanted to be king.

J He thought he was better than Enkidu.

25 How did Enkidu change after meeting Shamhat?

A from noble to selfish

B from brave to cowardly

C from untamed to mannerly

D from peace-loving to warlike

STOP

Part 2: Listening and Writing

Directions

In this part of the test, you will listen to two articles: "Comets" and "Asteroids." Then you will answer some questions to show how well you understood what was read.

For this practice test, ask a parent or friend to read the articles aloud twice. As you listen carefully, you may take notes on the articles during the readings. You may use these notes to answer the questions that follow. Use the space on pages 168 and 169 for your notes.

These articles are about two kinds of formations in space, comets and asteroids. These heavenly bodies are so similar that many people confuse the two, but there are differences between them, as you will learn.

Go On

Comets

People living on Earth thousands of years ago viewed comets in space. Chinese records dating back to 240 B.C.E. tell of "broom stars" sailing across the night sky. When people first saw comets, they were afraid of them and regarded them as evil omens foretelling impending doom. Astronomers today consider the sight of a comet an awesome opportunity to learn about space, having nothing to do with misfortune.

A comet has an orbit, much like a planet's orbit. A comet's orbit is much larger than a planet's, however, and extends far out into space, farther than Pluto, the planet with the greatest distance from the sun. When a comet is far from the sun, it appears to be nothing more than a space rock, but as the comet approaches the sun, its composition changes. A comet's center, or nucleus, consists of dust and rock particles, which are held together with ice. When the comet nears the sun, it heats up and the ice in its center melts. This causes gases to escape. The gases surround the comet forming a cloud, which is called the *coma*. The coma is surrounded by an arch of hydrogen. All of these gases glow, making the comet appear brilliant in the night sky. As the comet comes even closer to the sun, a stream of particles pushes away some of the gas. This pushed-away gas forms a long tail, which always points away from the sun.

Once the comet passes by the sun, it begins its orbit back out into the solar system. When a comet will be seen again depends on the size of its orbit. For example, while the comet Encke completes an orbit in only 3.30 years, the comet Hale-Bopp completes an orbit only every 4,000 years.

Go On

Asteroids

Asteroids are rocky metal-like space objects. It takes an asteroid about three to six years to orbit the sun. Asteroids can vary in size from small pebbles to minor planets. The asteroid Ceres, the first asteroid discovered, has a diameter of over 1,000 kilometers. Ceres is about the size of Texas! Some asteroids, like the asteroid Ida, even have tiny asteroid "moons" that orbit them. Asteroids that orbit other asteroids are referred to as *captured asteroids*. Scientists believe there are about 40,000 asteroids that are over 1 kilometer in size, but only about 3,000 of these have been catalogued, meaning their characteristics have been documented by astronomers.

While asteroids can be found anywhere in space, most are located within the *main belt*, also called the *asteroid belt*, an area between the orbits of Mars and Jupiter. Spacecraft traveling to the main belt have discovered that the asteroids there are actually very far apart and not close together the way they are depicted in science-fiction movies.

The Asteroid Belt

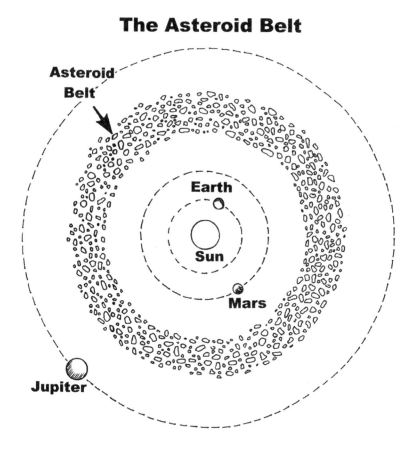

Rarely, an asteroid's orbit crosses Earth's orbit and collides with the Earth. Asteroids that will one day land on Earth are called *meteoroids*. Scientists are very interested in studying the composition of meteoroids since they have existed since the very early years of the solar system.

Go On

Notes

Notes

STOP

26 In the chart below, briefly describe the way people view comets now, and the way they viewed comets in ancient times. Use information from the "Comets" article in your answer.

Modern Times	Ancient Times

27 "Asteroids" describes a location in the solar system where asteroids are most likely to be found. Use information from the "Asteroids" article to describe this place and the discoveries scientists have made about it.

_____

_____

_____

_____

_____

_____

Go On

28 What are some similarities and differences between comets and asteroids? Use information from both articles to support your answer.

_____

_____

_____

_____

_____

_____

Go On

Planning Page

You may PLAN your writing for Number 29 here if you wish.

29

> Describe what a trip to space to observe comets and asteroids might be like.
>
> **In your answer, be sure to include**
> - how and when you might expect to see a comet
> - the appearance and location of an asteroid
> - information from BOTH articles

Check your writing for correct spelling, grammar, and punctuation.

_____

_____

_____

_____

_____

_____

_____

_____

_____

_____

_____

_____

_____

Go On

Sojourner Truth: Traveling Preacher

From its beginning, Isabella Baumfree's life was shrouded in hardship. She was denied freedom, separated from her parents, and treated like other people's property. Nobody could have imagined that, years later, she would assume the role of a powerful leader under the name Sojourner Truth.

In 1797, before slavery was abolished in all northern states of America, Baumfree was born into slavery in New York. Since her parents were slaves, she was forced to inherit that horrible destiny. As a young woman she was taken from her family and auctioned to different owners.

One of her owners arranged for her to marry another slave, named Thomas, and together they had five children. These children were in turn considered slaves, and most were taken away and sold just as Isabella and her siblings had been. Isabella could no longer tolerate the suffering. She snatched up her smallest child, abandoned Thomas, and escaped her enslavement.

In 1827, shortly after her escape, the state of New York emancipated its slaves. Isabella, Thomas, and all of their children were finally free. However, that announcement did little to alleviate their troubles. To earn a living, Isabella had to become a house servant for the Van Wagenen family. She even used their name temporarily. During her employment with the Wagenens, Isabella discovered that one of her previous owners had illegally sold her son to a slaveholder in Alabama. She recognized the crime that had been committed and courageously chose to bring the case to court. The court ruled in her favor and forced the crooked slave owners to release her son.

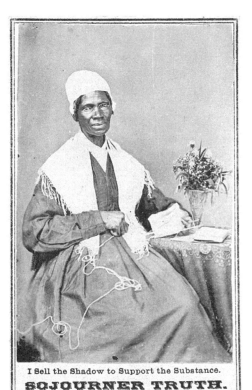

I Sell the Shadow to Support the Substance.
SOJOURNER TRUTH.

This was Isabella's first taste of empowerment. She'd defended her cause successfully. Now she was determined to spread that power to other black people and women who, at the time, had very little power to speak of.

Isabella was an ideal leader. She was about six feet tall, an exceptional height for a man or woman in her day. She also had developed muscular arms and shoulders from hundreds of days spent plowing fields. Her voice was remarkably deep, but she tempered it with her beautiful singing. Although she was illiterate, she was intelligent, humorous, and well-spoken.

She found additional motivation in religion, joining various communes and movements and studying their beliefs. In 1843, she renamed herself Sojourner Truth. A sojourner is a temporary resident; with her new name, she announced her new role as a traveling preacher.

Soon, Sojourner Truth had become famous for her speeches on women's rights and anti-slavery topics. Her most well-known speech is remembered for its dominant

Go On

challenge: "Ain't I a Woman?" She delivered this speech in 1851 at the Women's Convention in Akron, Ohio. In it, she linked the plight of black people in the south with the plight of white women in the north, and called for change. This is part of what Sojourner told her audience:

"That man over there says that women need to be helped into carriages, and lifted over ditches, and to have the best place everywhere. Nobody ever helps me into carriages, or over mud puddles, or gives me any best place—and ain't I a woman? Look at me. Look at my arm! I have plowed and planted, and gathered into barns, and no man could head me—and ain't I a woman? I could work as much and eat as much as a man, when I could get it, and bear the lash as well—and ain't I a woman? I have borne thirteen children, and seen most all sold off to slavery, and when I cried out with my mother's grief, none but Jesus heard me—and ain't I a woman?"

While Sojourner was extremely intelligent, she always expressed herself in a straight-forward manner. She concluded her legendary speech by simply saying, "Obliged to you for hearing me, and now old Sojourner ain't got nothing more to say."

The start of the Civil War in 1861 brought many of Sojourner's major concerns to the forefront. However, while the slavery question was being settled on battlefields across the nation, she was planning for life after the war.

By the time Sojourner Truth died in 1883, her contributions had given Americans many new ideas for the future. She was definitely a person ahead of her time. Sojourner spoke out for women's suffrage (voting rights) approximately 70 years before women gained the legal right to vote. She supported the temperance movement, which urged the government to put restrictions on alcohol, at least 50 years before the government decided to attempt it. She even personally challenged Abraham Lincoln to end segregation on street cars in 1864—which was 91 years before Rosa Parks sparked the modern civil rights movement by refusing to give up her seat on a city bus to a white person.

Go On

30 How did Sojourner Truth prove that women could be more powerful than people might have thought at the time? Use information from "Sojourner Truth: Traveling Preacher" to support your answer.

_____

_____

_____

_____

_____

_____

Go On

The First Emancipation

AM I NOT A MAN AND A BROTHER?

In January 1863, during the Civil War, President Abraham Lincoln delivered the Emancipation Proclamation. This speech officially declared the end of slavery in America. The southern states, which considered themselves a separate nation, refused to heed Lincoln's words. However, when the war ended and the United States of America was restored, Lincoln's message of freedom applied to every state. Finally the ancient institution of slavery was demolished in America.

For his heroic achievement, Lincoln has been dubbed "The Great Emancipator." However, many people don't realize that there were emancipations in America long before 1865.

As far back as the 1600s, when Europeans began to colonize America, slavery was considered normal. Many countries participated in the international slave trade, and thousands of slaves were brought to the New World. At first, many slaves were treated more as indentured servants. This meant that they were forced to do labor, but were given freedom after a certain period of time. Later, slavery was officially legalized by the colonies. Then, these servants were considered true slaves, property of their masters.

In the 1700s, slavery was common in the North. New England, the northeastern region of the country, was actually the center of the American slave trade. Thousands of slaves were employed there in farms, docks, and shipbuilding yards. However, as the end of that century drew near, slavery in the North was shaken by the American Revolution.

When America's Founding Fathers began struggling to free the nation from the tyranny of the British, they realized a great irony. American Nathaniel Niles summarized the problem when he said: "Let us either cease to enslave our fellow men, or else let us cease to complain of those that would enslave us." How could a nation proclaiming all men to be equal continue to allow slavery? During the course of the Revolutionary War, slavery in the North slowly but surely collapsed.

Go On

There are many reasons why slavery was abandoned in the North around the time of the war. One reason was that Britain was making money from the international slave trade. By refusing to purchase slaves, Americans were keeping money from the British. There was also growing pressure from religious groups, most notably the Quakers, who condemned slavery and insisted that it be ceased.

The final, killing blow to slavery in the North came during the battles of the Revolution. During the raging conflicts in the northern colonies, both the American and the British armies competed for the support of slaves. Many American colonies declared that any slave who would fight the British would be made free; the British in turn offered freedom to slaves who fought the Americans. Thousands of slaves participated in the Revolutionary War, on both sides, and were freed. Thousands more fled from their owners during the chaotic conflict.

Between 1777 and 1804, all of the colonies in the North finally abandoned the terrible institution of slavery. It would take nearly another hundred years, and another bloody war, to end slavery across all of America.

TIMELINE:

1776 – The Quakers in England and Pennsylvania require that members of their church free their slaves.

1777 – Slavery is banned in Vermont.

1780 – Massachusetts declares all men free and equal, including former slaves.

1780 – Pennsylvania passes a law to free slaves gradually.

1784 – Connecticut and Rhode Island choose to free slaves gradually.

1799 – New York follows Pennsylvania, Connecticut, and Rhode Island.

1807 – Federal law makes it illegal for Americans to participate in the slave trade.

Go On

31　Complete the chart below by writing three events from the passage that occurred between the two that are shown.

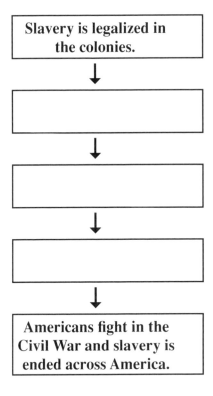

Slavery is legalized in
the colonies.

↓

↓

↓

↓

Americans fight in the
Civil War and slavery is
ended across America.

32　How did Britain affect the course of slavery in America? Use details from the article to support your answer.

_____

_____

_____

_____

_____

_____

Go On

Planning Page

You may PLAN your writing for Number 33 here if you wish, but do NOT write your final answer on this page. Your writing on this Planning Page will NOT count toward your final score. Write your final answer on pages 182 through 183.

33

Compare and contrast the struggles of the colonists with the struggles of Sojourner Truth. Use information in BOTH passages to support your answer.

In your answer, be sure to include
- how their struggles were similar
- how their struggles were different
- details from BOTH articles

Check your writing for correct spelling, grammar, and punctuation.

_____

_____

_____

_____

_____

_____

_____

_____

_____

_____

_____

_____

Go On

_Go On_

Planning Page

You may PLAN your writing for Number 34 here if you wish, but do NOT write your final answer on this page. Your writing on this Planning Page will NOT count toward your final score. Write your final answer on pages 185 through 186.

34

> The road from slavery to equality was a long one for African Americans. Write an essay in which you discuss why you think it took almost one hundred years for African Americans to gain rights equal to those of white Americans.
>
> In your essay, be sure to include
> - how you think the country reacted to the end of slavery
> - how you think the country reacted to the end of segregation
> - details about what may have happened in between

Check your writing for correct spelling, grammar, and punctuation.

_____

_____

_____

_____

_____

_____

_____

_____

_____

_____

_____

_____

Go On

STOP

MARKING INSTRUCTIONS

Make heavy BLACK marks.
Erase cleanly.
Make no stray marks.

●

CORRECT
MARK

INCORRECT
MARK

Multiple-choice questions

1. Ⓐ Ⓑ Ⓒ Ⓓ

2. Ⓕ Ⓖ Ⓗ Ⓙ

3. Ⓐ Ⓑ Ⓒ Ⓓ

4. Ⓕ Ⓖ Ⓗ Ⓙ

5. Ⓐ Ⓑ Ⓒ Ⓓ

6. Ⓕ Ⓖ Ⓗ Ⓙ

7. Ⓐ Ⓑ Ⓒ Ⓓ

8. Ⓕ Ⓖ Ⓗ Ⓙ

9. Ⓐ Ⓑ Ⓒ Ⓓ

10. Ⓕ Ⓖ Ⓗ Ⓙ

11. Ⓐ Ⓑ Ⓒ Ⓓ

12. Ⓕ Ⓖ Ⓗ Ⓙ

13. Ⓐ Ⓑ Ⓒ Ⓓ

14. Ⓕ Ⓖ Ⓗ Ⓙ

15. Ⓐ Ⓑ Ⓒ Ⓓ

16. Ⓕ Ⓖ Ⓗ Ⓙ

17. Ⓐ Ⓑ Ⓒ Ⓓ

18. Ⓕ Ⓖ Ⓗ Ⓙ

19. Ⓐ Ⓑ Ⓒ Ⓓ

20. Ⓕ Ⓖ Ⓗ Ⓙ

21. Ⓐ Ⓑ Ⓒ Ⓓ

22. Ⓕ Ⓖ Ⓗ Ⓙ

23. Ⓐ Ⓑ Ⓒ Ⓓ

24. Ⓕ Ⓖ Ⓗ Ⓙ

25. Ⓐ Ⓑ Ⓒ Ⓓ

Student Name_____

Posttest—Part 1

1. **B** understand stated information

   This answer is stated in the passage. A beaded cape covered Queen Puabi's body.

2. **H** identify main idea

   Most of paragraph two is about the royal tombs in the cemetery. The paragraph discusses the kings, queens, and their families buried in the tombs. Answer choice H is the best answer.

3. **A** understand stated information

   This answer is stated in the passage. The Sumerians believed that their kings were gods, and they built elaborate burial chambers to please them.

4. **H** identify author's point of view/purpose

   This question asks you to identify the author's purpose. While answer choice G might seem to be correct, the passage does more than teach readers about Queen Puabi's tomb. It informs readers about the Royal Cemetery at Ur.

5. **A** draw conclusions and make inferences

   The passage says that the king's tomb was looted, most likely when they buried the queen, whose chamber was on top of him. This leads you to conclude that the queen's tomb would have been at great risk of being robbed if another body had been buried on top of her chamber. Answer choice A is the best answer.

6. **G** use critical analysis

   You have to understand the poem to correctly answer this question. The poet is looking at his reflection in a mirror.

7. **C** interpret characters

   The man in the looking glass is a faithful companion to the man. Answer choice C is correct.

8. **H** interpret plot

   The man in the looking glass goes with the poet when he is alone. This is stated in the poem.

9. **D** interpret literary devices

   This question asks you about the tone of the poem. You can reach this answer by process of elimination. The tone is not really weary, angry, or relieved. It is speculative.

10. **J** interpret plot

    The poet loses everything but himself. He states this in the last line of the poem. Answer choice J is the correct answer.

11. **D** draw conclusions and make inferences

    The passage says that the concession stands were responsible for a large amount of the profits made by drive-in theaters, so you can conclude that answer choice D, money spent on food and drinks, is the best answer.

12. **G** use critical analysis

    This question asks you to select an opinion. Remember that an opinion is what someone thinks. Answer choice G, "These families will treasure the experience as much as those of the past," is the author's opinion.

13. **D** understand stated information

The answer to this question is in the passage. In the 1980s people did not visit drive-in theaters because they had VCRs in their home. You can find this answer under the subheading, "Drive-in Theaters Hit a Roadblock."

14. **H** use critical analysis

This question asks you to choose the answer choice that shows that an effort was made to make drive-in theaters more family friendly. The best answer is H, which says that theater owners built playgrounds where children could play before the movie started. While answer choice J might also seem correct because it says carhops brought food to cars' windows, this doesn't relate specifically to families.

15. **D** use critical analysis

To answer this question correctly, you have to select an answer choice that faded in popularity. Movies, fast food, and the Internet are still popular. Therefore, the correct answer choice is D, radio dramas.

16. **F** identify author's point of view/purpose

This question asks you the purpose of the flyer. This flyer informs the public about an "upcoming event," a microchip clinic.

17. **C** use critical analysis

This question asks you about the organization of the flyer. The flyer sorts topics under headings. Therefore, answer choice C is the correct answer.

18. **F** understand stated information

To answer this question correctly, you have to find the information that is not stated in the passage. The flyer does not give you a name of a contact person, so answer choice F is the correct answer.

19. **D** interpret plot

This question asks you about the plot of the story. You have to interpret the story correctly to answer this question. Gilgamesh began to respect Enkidu after he learned that he was a great warrior.

20. **J** interpret plot

You can answer this question correctly by rereading the beginning of the passage. The people of Babylon were upset with King Gilgamesh because he continually interfered in wedding ceremonies.

21. **B** draw conclusions/make inferences

You won't find the answer to this question stated in the passage. You have to draw a conclusion. The author records Gilgamesh's thoughts after he speaks with his mother to explain his immediate reaction.

22. **F** use text to understand vocabulary

The word cession means "end," so answer choice F is the correct answer. The people celebrated the end of the threat.